Occasional Papers, By C.H.M.

Charles Henry Mackintosh

OCCASIONAL PAPERS.

BY

C. H. M.

"Feed the flock of God."—1 *Pet.* v. 2.

LONDON:
W. H. BROOM, 28, PATERNOSTER ROW;
G. MORRISH, 24, WARWICK LANE.
1867.

PREFACE.

The title of this little volume so exactly expresses what the reader is to expect therein, that little is needed in the way of preface. However, it may be well to state that some of the following papers appeared many years ago in periodicals which are now out of print. Others appeared more recently in a separate form. The publisher requested permission to publish all in one volume; and the writer, seeing no just ground for refusing, gave his consent. May the Lord affix the seal of His approval! Nothing less will do; nothing more is needed.

C. H. M.

26, Portland Square, Bristol,
November, 1867.

OCCASIONAL PAPERS.

THE PRISONER OF HOPE.

Zechariah ix. 12.

There are two leading principles in the soul of the Christian, which make God the special object. These are "faith and hope." There is a marked distinction, and yet an intimate connection, between these two principles. Faith takes what God has given; hope expects what He has promised. Faith rests in holy tranquillity in God's statements about the *past;* hope goes forth in active longings after the *future.* Faith is a recipient; hope an expectant. Now, it will be found that, in proportion to the vigour of faith, will be the vigour of hope. If we be not "fully persuaded that what God has promised, He is able also to perform," we shall know but little of the power or energy of hope. If faith be wavering, hope will be flickering. On the contrary, if faith be strong, hope will be strong also; for faith, while it nourishes and strengthens the persuasion, imparts strength and intensity to the expectation. Thus, the soul, in the happy exercise of the above principles, is like a climbing plant which, striking its roots downward into the soil, sends forth its tendrils along the nearest wall or tree. So the soul finds its root in the eternal record of God, while it sends forth the tendrils of an imperishable hope to grasp tenaciously the faithful promise of God; and, we may say, the deeper the root, the stronger the tendril.

The patriarch Abraham was a happy exemplification of all this; his "faith and hope" were truly "in God." Circumstances added nothing to him. He had been promised the whole land of Canaan, where he had not so much as to set his foot on; he had been promised a seed like the stars of heaven, or like the sand by the sea shore, when as yet he had no child. Thus, neither his faith nor his hope could have drawn any nutriment from circumstances, for everything within the range of mortal vision argued against him. But the promise of "the Almighty God" was quite enough for the man of faith. With nought but that, he started forth as a pilgrim and a stranger, having no foundation for his hopes that could at all be recognised by "flesh and blood." Abraham had heard a voice which the children of this world could not hear, even the voice of "the God of glory," calling him forth from the midst of his worldly circumstances to be "a prisoner of hope." The Lord had directed his thoughts upward—He had called him from earth to heaven—from the earthly Babel to the heavenly Jerusalem—from the baseless city of man, to the well-founded city of God.

Thus was it with all the patriarchs and witnesses whose honoured names the Spirit has recorded, for our encouragement, in Hebrews xi. "They all died in faith, not having received the promises, but having seen them afar off, and were persuaded of them, and embraced them, and confessed that they were strangers and pilgrims on the earth." They died as they had lived, "prisoners of hope." An unbelieving world might scoff and sneer at them, and wonder why they had given up the apparently substantial realities of earth to live and die without anything. But their "faith and hope" were in God, and not in circumstances. Faith enabled them to rest with tranquillized spirits upon the record of God, while hope carried them onward into the future, and converted it into the present.

But the verse which stands at the head of this paper presents the believer in two most interesting aspects, viz., as the recipient of *grace*, and the expectant of *glory*—as one safely lodged in a "stronghold," but yet as "a prisoner of hope" —as one in the enjoyment of perfect peace, and also living in the blessed hope of better things. These two points may afford matter for profitable reflection, through the Lord's mercy.

There is only one thing that can render the soul happy in looking forward into the future, and that is, the knowledge of God's redeeming love in giving His Son to be a perfect sacrifice for sin. Until this is known, the mind will never reach beyond the question of mere individual salvation, which, after all, is but selfishness. The human heart is, in a measure, conscious that all is not right with it, and hence it is ill at ease at the thought of the future. "It is appointed unto men once to die, and after that the judgment." Death and judgment form a gloomy prospect for man to contemplate. Death draws aside the curtain and reveals the terrible future—it launches the poor soul forth into the boundless ocean of eternity, without anything to sustain or guide it. But "the one offering of Jesus Christ" brings the soul into new ground, alters its point of view, and removes the clouds from the prospect. "So," says the apostle, "Christ was once offered to bear the sins of many; and unto them that look for Him shall He appear the second time without sin unto salvation" (Heb. ix. 28). The sinner must get at the other side of the cross ere he can happily or peacefully look forward. In other words, we can only study prophecy with a purged conscience. It is when we know, through the Spirit, the value of the sufferings of Christ, that we can joyfully contemplate the glory that is to follow. The unconverted, therefore, have nothing to do with prophecy. To them the throne from whence Jehovah reveals His deep counsels is surrounded with thick clouds and darkness, and sends forth nothing but thunderings and lightnings. The prophetic book is sealed with seven seals, and none but *the Lamb* can open it.

If, then, it be true that a purged conscience is

needful ere prophecy can be rightly studied, we need not wonder that so little is known about it by those who consider it the highest point of Christian attainment to be able to feel that the conscience is cleansed from every stain. Until the grand doctrine of forgiveness—full, free, and eternal forgiveness—is known as the unquestionable portion of the soul, through the finished work of the Lamb of God, no marvel that every other question, be it ever so important, should be held in abeyance. The value and efficacy of *grace* must be known ere *glory* is thought of. That grace which brings salvation must first be received before "the blessed hope" can be enjoyed.

All this leads us to see the distinction between the work of the evangelist and that of the teacher. The evangelist should lead the sinner to see that the work on which his soul is to rest has been accomplished, and that he cannot, by any possibility, add thereto. He has to convey a simple message concerning an accomplished work, which work must be the basis of the poor guilty sinner's peace. He does not assume anything with respect to those to whom he speaks, but that they are dead in trespasses and sins—dead as Ezekiel's valley of dry bones, and as unable to live or move. The evangelist is privileged to stand in the midst of a ruined, self-destroyed, guilty world; and there to offer salvation, in the name of his Master, to all who will believe the word concerning the cross. It is of the utmost importance that all who occupy the position of evangelists should clearly understand the nature and limits of their work, and the terms of their commission. It too often happens that preachers of the gospel mar their work by intruding upon the province of the teacher. They think it incumbent on them to press upon the attention of people the fruits that result from the reception of the gospel, lest they should be suspected of antinomianism. This is, properly speaking, the work of the teacher, who has to do only with those who have passed under the hand of the evangelist. The teacher has no more to do with *sinners* than the evangelist has to do with *saints*.*

Nor is the teacher to confine himself to the matter of pressing upon the conscience of the believer his responsibilities; he has also to instruct him in the nature of his hope, he has to expound to him the book of prophecy, according to the wisdom of the Holy Ghost. The evangelist has to speak of what God *has* done; the teacher, of what He *will* do. The former calls for the action of faith; the latter, for the action of hope—the former points to the stronghold; the latter speaks to the prisoner of hope. If these things be confounded, the effect will be most pernicious. It is as wrong for the unbeliever to be addressed on the

* Of course, we may often see the gift of an evangelist and a teacher developed in the same person. Where they are thus combined, great care is needed not to confound them in their exercise.

subject of the hopes of the Church, as it is for the believer to be confined to the question of the forgiveness of sins. The enemy of souls may often work.much mischief by leading the unregenerate to exercise their intellects on the subject of prophecy. He is doing so at the present day, seeing he has not been able to prevent Christians from searching into their Father's testimonies concerning the future. The devil will endeavour either to suppress or corrupt the truth of God. For ages he succeeded in keeping the Church of Christ from the perception of the precious doctrine of the coming of the Lord; and now that attention has been awakened on the subject, he is maliciously seeking to nullify it by causing unhallowed lips to proclaim and teach it, or by causing Christians to differ about it.

Now, the remedy for both these dangerous evils is the simple understanding of the Christian's place, as a prisoner of hope. It is not to amuse the intellect, nor to please the fancy, that the Spirit of God has spoken of the Church's destinies. No; it is for the purpose of comforting the prisoner, by giving him a well-grounded hope. Nor is it for any, save those who find themselves within the stronghold of the blood-stricken door, that the prospect of rest and glory has been painted in the distance. Looking at the believer in one aspect of his character, he is like the Israelite within the blessed circle of peace which redemption had described around him, feeding on the Lamb whose blood had secured his peace, with girded loins, waiting for the first beams of the morning, to leave the land of death and darkness to proceed on his way toward the land of rest. So the believer, resting in the atoning efficacy of the blood of Christ, is privileged to look forward to "the morning without clouds," not that he may then know, for the first time, that he is accepted in the Beloved, but that he may enter into all the rich and ineffable fruits of redeeming love. Thus, the believer is a prisoner of hope. His faith reposes on the cross—his hope feeds upon the rich pastures of God's prophetic record. His spirit travels over a course of which the cross is the starting-post, and glory the goal. He finds it

> "Sweet to look back and see his name
> In life's fair book set down;
> Sweet to look forward and behold
> Eternal joys his own."

The two points are inseparable. It is only when we find it sweet to look back, that we also find it sweet to look forward. We must see our names in the fair book of life, written there in indelible characters, before we can understand our title to eternal joys. It is impossible that any one can rightly enter upon the investigation of the doctrine of the hopes of the Church, until his spirit has been perfectly tranquillized by the blood of atonement. To the unwashed soul the prospect is unspeakably dreadful. "Enter not into judgment with Thy servant, O Lord, for in Thy sight shall no flesh living be justified." Prophecy conveys a twofold message; it tells of unmitigated judgment to the man who is yet in his sins; and it tells of incorruptibility and eternal life to the man who has believed in the love of God as displayed in the gift of His Son. Hence, to the former, it must be a most unwelcome messenger; to the latter, the bearer of most gladsome tidings: to the former it speaks of the complete shipwreck; to the latter, the glorious consummation of all his hopes.

The children of this world are not prisoners of hope, they are prisoners under condemnation; they wait, not to be emancipated, but to be executed; it is not endless rest, but endless torment, that lies before them. Miserable prospect! O ye men of this world, what will it be when your cup of pleasure shall be dashed from your lips for ever? when the world, that idol for which you have lived and laboured, and at whose altar you have sacrificed everything, shall pass away into everlasting destruction? What would you not then give to find yourselves in a stronghold—even in the stronghold which faith finds in the sacrifice of Christ? It is nothing but the blindest infatuation to give up God's future for man's present—to sell the coming glory of Christ for the present glory of the world. Far better to endure the temporary privations of a prisoner's life here, than to suffer an eternal imprisonment with Satan and his angels. Poor sinner, the crucified Jesus calls upon you to "turn to the stronghold;" to take refuge, by faith, beneath the shadow of the cross, and there to wait, as a prisoner of hope, for the glory which shall speedily be revealed from heaven. And you, Christian reader, who have, through grace, found rest for your wearied spirit, do you seek to know more of what is involved in that title, "a prisoner of hope."

We can form some idea of the intensity of a prisoner's longing for the day of release; we may imagine how eagerly a prisoner of old would long to hear the soul-stirring note of the trumpet of jubilee, announcing his complete deliverance from captivity. We know full well that it is not with the gloomy and crumbling walls of his prison-house that the prisoner engages his attention; he seeks not to decorate or render them stable. No; he groans and sighs for deliverance. Just so should it ever be with us. We should unceasingly "groan within ourselves, waiting for the adoption, to wit, the redemption of our body." "We," says the apostle, "that are in this tabernacle, do groan, being burdened; not that we would be unclothed, but clothed upon, that mortality might be swallowed up of life."

Here is the proper language of a prisoner of hope. It is not merely groaning to be set free from the cage in which we are pent up, but "to be clothed upon with our house which is from heaven." Doubtless, we feel the sorrow and trial of our present position; we are made to taste the irksomeness and roughness of the journey; we are called to enter into the painfulness of being imprisoned in a body of sin and death. In a word, "we groan, being burdened." Nevertheless, the putting off of the earthly tabernacle would not perfectly remedy the case. To be unclothed as to our spirits would not make us perfectly happy. Very many Christians err in their thoughts on this subject. They think that the moment the spirit escapes from its prison-house, it enters into perfect bliss. That such is not the case, the passage just quoted most fully proves. Nothing can fill up the measure of the believer's joy, but his being clothed upon with his house which is from heaven; for, until then, whether he be imprisoned in the tomb, or in a body of sin and death, death and mortality bear sway, so far as the body is concerned; but when he appears in his resurrection garments of glory and beauty, death shall have been swallowed up in victory, and mortality swallowed up of life. To speak of perfect bliss, while the spirit is unclothed and the body mingled with the dust, is a contradiction.

There are, I believe, but four places in the New Testament where the state of the unclothed spirit is spoken of, and in none of these have we anything approaching to a full description of that state. When contrasting it with our present painful and trying condition, the apostle says, "*it is far better.*" Yes, truly, it is "far better" to be at rest from our labours than toiling here—far better to be away from a scene of strife and turmoil, where everything tends to draw out the vileness of nature. But all this would not constitute the summit of blessedness. How very differently the Holy Ghost speaks of the resurrection state! It would be out of the question to think of citing, or even referring to, the various passages in which this glorious subject is treated of. The New Testament abounds with them. Nor is there any mystery or vagueness in the manner in which it is put before us. No; we are clearly, explicitly, and simply taught that the resurrection and the glories connected with it will constitute the very consummation of the believer's joy and blessedness; and, moreover, that, until then, he is but a prisoner of hope. The patriarchs, the prophets, the apostles, the noble army of martyrs—all our beloved brethren who have gone before us—yea, and the Master Himself—all wait for the morning of resurrection. "These all, having obtained a good report, through faith, received not the promise: God having provided some better thing for us, that they, *without us*, should not be made perfect." God must gather His family together—the grave must let go from its grasp every redeemed one—every scattered member of the flock of Christ must be gathered into the heavenly fold ere the festivities of the kingdom can commence.

Thus we see the vast importance of being rightly instructed as to the nature of our hope. When we know what we are hoping for, we are able to give an answer; yea, our lives answer. *A man's life is always influenced by his genuine hopes.* If a man be an heir to an estate, his life is influenced by the hope of inheriting it; and if we knew more of the power of the Spirit as "the earnest of our inheritance," instead of disputing about the time or manner of our Master's arrival, we should, as "*prisoners of hope,*" be anxiously looking forth from our prison windows, and saying, "Why is His chariot so long in coming? Why tarry the wheels of His chariot?"

Oh! that all who have found a stronghold in the cross of Jesus may say more earnestly, "Come, Lord Jesus, come quickly."

JACOB ALONE WITH GOD.

Genesis xxxii. 24–32.

In tracing the history of Jacob, and in contemplating his natural character, we are again and again reminded of the grace expressed in those words, "*Jacob have I loved.*" The question why God should love such a one, can only receive for an answer the boundless and sovereign grace of Him who sets His love upon objects possessing nothing of worth in themselves, and "who calls things that be not as though they were that no flesh should glory in His presence." Jacob's natural character was most unamiable; his name indeed was at once the expression of what he was—"*a supplanter.*" He commenced his course in the development of this, his disposition, and until thoroughly crushed, as in these verses, he pursued a course of the merest bargain-making. On leaving his father's house, he makes a bargain with God. "If God," says he, "will be with me, and will keep me in this way that I go, and will give me bread to eat, and raiment to put on, so that I come again to my father's house in peace; then shall the Lord be my God; and this stone, which I have set for a pillar, shall be God's house, and of all that Thou shalt give me I will surely give the tenth unto Thee" (Gen. xxviii. 20–22). Here we find him making a bargain with God Himself, the full evidence of what his real character was. Then again, mark him during the period of his sojourn with Laban; see there, what plans, what deep-laid schemes to promote his own ends. How plainly it is seen that *self* was the grand object before his mind, in all that he put his hand to. So it is in the course of this thirty-second chapter. He is deeply engaged in plans to turn away the dreaded wrath of his more manly, though badly treated, brother Esau.

But there is one circumstance with regard to Jacob in this chapter which deserves attention. He is seen labouring under the painful effects of a bad conscience, with regard to his brother; he knew that he had acted towards him in a way calculated to call out his anger and revenge, and he is therefore ill at ease at the prospect of meeting him. But *God* had a controversy with Jacob. He had to lead him through a course of education that was to teach him that "all flesh is grass." Jacob thought only of appeasing Esau by a present. True, he turns aside, in this chapter, to offer up confession and prayer, yet notwithstanding, it is manifest that his heart was engaged about his *own* arrangements for appeasing Esau, more than anything else. But God was looking at him in all this, and preparing a salutary course of discipline for him, in order to teach him what was in his heart. For this purpose was "Jacob *left alone.*" All his company, arranged according to his own plan, had passed on, and he himself was awaiting this much dreaded interview with no small degree of anxiety. There is peculiar force in the words, "*Jacob was left alone.*" Thus is it with all who have been trained in the school of God; they have been brought into the stillness and solitude of the Divine presence, there to view themselves and their ways, where alone they can be rightly viewed. Had Jacob continued amid the bleating of the sheep, and the lowing of the oxen, he could not by any means have enjoyed the same calm and sober view of himself and his past course, as he was led to in the secret of the presence of God. "*Jacob was left alone.*" Oh! there is no part of a man's history so important as when he is thus led into the solitude of the Divine presence; it is there he understands things which were before dark and inexplicable. There he can judge of men and things in their proper light; there, too, he can judge of self, and see its proper nothingness and vileness.

In Psalm lxxiii. we find a soul looking abroad upon the world and reasoning upon what he saw there,—reasoning to such an extent, that he was almost tempted to say it was vain to serve the Lord at all.

In Psalm lxxvii. we find a soul looking *inward*, and reasoning upon what he saw *within*,—reasoning to such an extent as to question the continuance of God's grace. What was the remedy in both cases? "*The sanctuary.*" I went into the sanctuary of God; and then understood. So it was with Jacob; his "sanctuary" was the lonely spot, where God wrestled with him until the breaking of the day.

The careful reader will find that this passage, when taken as it stands, affords no foundation for the popular idea, namely, that it furnishes an instance of Jacob's power in prayer. That no such idea is set forth will at once appear from the expression, "*There wrestled a man with him;*" it is not said that *he* wrestled with the man, which would give an entirely different aspect to the scene. I believe that, so far from its proving Jacob's power in prayer, it rather proves the tenacity with which he grasped the flesh, and the things thereof. So firmly indeed did he hold fast his "confidence in the flesh," that all night long the struggle continued. "The supplanter" held out, nor did he yield until the very seat of his strength was touched, and he was made to feel indeed that "all flesh is grass."

Such is the obvious teaching of this very important Scripture. Instead of Jacob's patience and perseverance in prayer, we have God's patience in dealing with one who needed to have his "*old man*" crushed to the very dust, ere God could make anything of him. This momentous scene gives us the grand turning point in the life of this extraordinary man. We are here reminded of Saul's conversion; Jacob, with the hollow of his thigh touched, like Saul, prostrate in the dust, between Jerusalem and Damascus. We observe, on the one hand, the broken fragments of "a supplanter," and the elements of God's mighty "Prince;" on the other hand, the fragments of a persecutor and injurious one, and the elements of God's mighty apostle.

And we may ask, What means the expression, "I will not let Thee go except Thou bless me"? What, but the utterance of one that had made the wondrous discovery that he was "without strength"? Jacob was let into the secret of *human weakness*, and therefore felt that it must be *Divine strength* or nothing. He thinks no more of his goodly plans and arrangements, his presents to appease my lord Esau. No; he stands withered and trembling before *the One* who had humbled him, and cries, "I will not let *Thee* go except Thou bless me." Surely, this is the gate of heaven! Jacob had, as it were, arrived at the end of *flesh;* it is no longer "*me*" but "*Thee.*" He clings to Christ as the poor shipwrecked mariner clings to the rock. All self-confidence is gone, all expectations from self and the world blasted, every chain of self-devised security dissolved like a morning cloud before the beams of the sun. All his bargains availed him nothing at all. How miserable must everything that ever he did have seemed to him; yea, even his offer to give a tenth to God, when thus laid in the dust of self-abasement and conscious weakness! The mighty wrestler says, "Let me go, for the day breaketh." What a striking expression, "Let me go." He was determined to make manifest the condition of Jacob's soul. If Jacob had without delay let go his grasp, he would have proved that his heart was still wrapped up in his worldly plans and schemes; but, on the contrary, when he cries out, "I will not let Thee go," he declares that God alone was the spring of all his soul's joy and strength; he, in effect, says, "Whom have I in heaven but *Thee?* and there is none upon earth I desire beside *Thee;*" or, with the twelve, in the sixth chapter of John: "Lord, to whom shall we go? Thou hast the words of eternal life."

Blessed experience! So is it with the poor convicted soul; he may have been trusting in his own righteousness, as Jacob was in his goodly, well-devised plans; he may have been building upon his moral life; but, oh! when once the arrow of conviction has pierced him, has laid open his very soul, and told him *all* that ever he did, he trusts in self *no longer*, but exclaims with Job, "Now mine eye hath seen *Thee;* wherefore I abhor myself, and repent in dust and ashes." "I will not let *Thee* go except Thou bless me." Such will ever be the happy effect of a thorough acquaintance with our own hearts. Jacob now gets his name changed: he must not be any longer known as "the supplanter," but as "*a prince*," having *power* with God through the very knowledge of his *weakness;* for, "when I am *weak*, then am I *strong*." We are never so strong as when we feel ourselves weak, even as "water spilt upon the ground, that cannot be gathered up again;" and, on the contrary, we are never so weak as when we fancy ourselves strong. Peter never displayed more lamentable weakness than when he fancied he had uncommon strength: had he felt somewhat of Jacob's happy condition when his sinew shrank, he would have thought, acted, and spoken differently.

We should not turn from this passage, without at least seeing distinctly what it was that gave Jacob "power with God and with man;" it was the full consciousness of his own nothingness. Who that hearkens for a moment to those precious words, "I will not let Thee go except Thou bless me," and beholds the humbled patriarch clinging closely to the One who had broken him down, can fail to see that Jacob's "*power*" consisted in his "*weakness*"? There is nothing here of Jacob's power in prayer. No: all we see is, first, Jacob's strength in the flesh, and God weakening him; then, his weakness in the flesh, and God strengthening him. This is indeed the great moral of the scene. Jacob was satisfied to go "*halting*" on his journey, seeing he had learnt the secret of *true* strength. He was able to move along, using the words afterwards uttered by St. Paul: "I will, therefore, gladly glory in my *infirmities*, that the *power of Christ* may rest upon me." Yes, "*my infirmities*" on the one hand, and "*the power of Christ*" on the other, will be found to constitute the sum total of the life of a Christian.

I would observe, that there seems to be a marked connection between the spirit of this instructive passage and that of Galatians vi. 16: "As many as walk according to *this rule*, peace be on them and mercy, and upon *the Israel of God*." What rule? "The cross of our Lord Jesus Christ." This is God's rule. It is not "circumcision or uncircumcision, but a new creature." (καινὴ κτίσις.) This the rule which distinguishes the Israel of God; this the grand distinction between "the supplanters" and "the princes:" the former trust in *the flesh*, the latter "*in the cross*." The Israel of God have ever been identified with weakness in themselves, like Jacob halting along, having the sentence of death written in their flesh. Thus the apostle goes on to say: "From henceforth let no one trouble me; for *I bear in my body* the marks of the Lord Jesus." (στίγματα τοῦ κυρίου.) So did Jacob bear in his "body the marks of the Lord Jesus." Nor was he at all ashamed of them; because, while they were at once the marks of *Jacob's weakness*, they were also the marks of *Israel's strength*. Blessed strength! May we know more and more of it daily!

I would only observe, in conclusion, that Esau was not met by *Jacob*, but by *Israel*, and as a consequence, all was peace and sunshine—the difficulty vanishes, the danger disappears. God, who had crushed Jacob's "*old man*," exercised an influence on Esau's mind, else the consequences might have been terrible. How happy it is for us when we can thus meet difficulties at the other side of the cross! Jacob had been *alone* with God, and could therefore be *alone* with Esau.

THE LOVE OF JESUS.

In looking at Revelation i. 5, 6, we can trace the following actings of love: first, love *thinks* of its objects. This marks the motive in operation to be unaffectedly pure, for when the heart regales itself by meditating on its object, it seeks not to be noticed, to be praised or exalted for thinking of its object; its reward is found in the very thought itself—a reward, a pleasure with which nothing can compare.

Secondly, love *visits* its object. It could not be content with merely thinking: the same principle that leads love to *think* with pleasure, induces it to *visit* its object; and, moreover, we can trace the same purity, elevation, and disinterestedness, in the visit as in *the thought*. It does not *think* upon its object in order to please or attract the attention of any one, neither does it *visit* in order to effect such ends; it has *its own real, substantial* enjoyment, both in thinking of and visiting *its object*.

Thirdly, love *suffers* for its object. It rests not satisfied with merely *thinking* of, or *visiting* its object—it *must suffer*. In order to exhibit itself in all its reality and intensity, love must put itself to cost for its object; it must spend and be spent, not because it expects a return, but simply because *it will* express itself in a way not to be mistaken. Love never thinks of what it may reap for itself in thus suffering. No: it simply contemplates *its object*, in thinking of, visiting, and suffering for it.

Fourthly, love *exalts* its object. This is the highest point. In the exaltation of its object, love sees the fruit of previous thought, visitation, and suffering. Hence, love feels exquisite happiness in exalting its object, for in so doing, it reaps the wished-for harvest.

Let us now apply the above blessed characteristics of love to the Lord Jesus, and see how His love exhibited all of them. Did not He ponder in His own eternal mind His much-loved Church before the foundation of the world? Yes, truly "His gracious eye surveyed us ere stars were seen above." Did He rest satisfied with merely thinking about us? No: He laid aside all His glory; He came down into this cold, heartless world, as into a vast quarry, from whence He hoped to hew out stones for the temple. He made His way down into this "*rough valley*" of ours, which had "neither been eared nor sown." "The day-spring from *on high* hath *visited* us;" but He did not rest satisfied with coming down to look at us in our misery and degradation; He determined to *suffer* for us, to groan, to bleed, to die for us; He hath washed us in "*His own blood*," which marks the intensity of His suffering for us. What, then, was all this for? Why those ineffable sufferings of Jesus? Why the groans and bloody sweat in he garden? Why the mysterious hour of profound darkness, together with the cry, "Why hast Thou forsaken me?" Simply that the love of Jesus might *exalt* its object. And He has exalted His object, yea, to the highest point of elevation: "He hath made us kings and priests unto God."

Thus we have seen how the love of Jesus has *thought* of, *visited*, *suffered* for, and *exalted* its object: this is for our comfort. But then we should remember that if we love Jesus, *we too* will often like to *think* of Him, to contemplate His grace, ponder over His perfections; moreover, we will pay frequent *visits* to the secret of His sanctuary, not to gain a name as persons of much prayer, but simply to indulge the desires of our hearts after Him "who is the fairest among ten thousand, and altogether lovely." Again, we shall be ready to *suffer* for Him, not in order to commend ourselves to our brethren as persons of great energy and zeal, but to express the high estimation in which we hold His blessed Person. Finally, it will be our constant effort to *exalt* Him in every place; our constant cry will be, "O magnify the Lord with me, and let us exalt His name together." Let us earnestly pray for such a deep tide of Divine love in our poor, cold, narrow, selfish hearts, as will make our service not the mere spurt of imperfect zeal, kindled by the unhallowed spark of human opinion, but the calm, steady, constant flow of unalterable affection for Jesus—that affection which has its primary joy in *pondering* over its object, ere it comes forth as an *actor* or a *sufferer* in *His cause.*

"Come, saints, praise the Lamb, His mercies proclaim,
And lift up your heads and sing of His name;
His love to the Church, which He purchased with blood,
To make her His bride and the temple of God."

FALSE WORSHIP.

Leviticus x. 1–11.

In meditating upon the ordinances of the Mosaic ritual, one thing in particular strikes the mind, viz., the remarkably jealous way in which God fenced Himself round from the approach of man, as such. It is salutary for the soul to ponder this. We are in great danger of admitting into our minds an element of unholy familiarity when thinking of God, which the devil may use in a very pernicious way and to a very evil end.

It is a fundamental principle of truth, that in proportion as God is exalted and reverenced in our thoughts, will our walk through life be shaped in accordance with what He loves and enjoins; in other words, there is a strong moral link between our estimate of God and our moral conduct. If our thoughts of God are *low*, low will be our standard of Christian walk; if high, the result will be accordingly. Thus, when Israel, at the foot of mount Horeb, "changed their glory into the similitude of an ox that eateth grass," the Lord's words were, "Thy people, which thou broughtest out of the land of Egypt, have *corrupted themselves.*" Mark those words, "corrupted themselves." They could not do otherwise, when they let down their thoughts of the dignity and majesty of God so low as to imagine, for a moment, that He was "like an ox that eateth grass."

Similar is the teaching of Romans i. There

the apostle shows us that the reason of all the abominations of the Gentile nations must be sought for in the fact, that "when they knew God, they glorified Him not *as God;*" thus they too "corrupted themselves." This is a principle possessing vast practical influence. If we attempt to lower God, we *must* necessarily lower ourselves; and herein we are furnished with a key by which to interpret all religion. There is an inseparable link between the character of the god of any religion and the character of the votaries thereof, and Jehovah was constantly reminding *His* people of the fact, that *their* conduct was to be the consequence of what *He* was. "I am the Lord thy God, that brought thee up out of the land of Egypt; therefore," etc., "be ye holy, for *I* am holy." And exactly similar is the Spirit's word to us: "He that hath this hope in him purifieth *himself*, even as *He* is pure."

This principle, I conceive, carries us far above all merely systematic views of truth; it is not at all a question of mere doctrine. No; it brings us at once into the deep recesses of the soul, there to ponder, as beneath the piercing, jealous eye of the *Thrice Holy One*, the estimate which we, as individuals, are daily and hourly forming of *Him*. I feel that we cannot with impunity refuse to give our minds seriously to this important point of truth; it will be found to contain much of the secret of our low walk and lamentable deadness. God is not exalted in our thoughts; *He* has not the supreme place in our affections; self, the world, our family, our daily employments, have, as regards the most of us, thrust down our gracious God from the throne of our affections, and robbed the One who died to save us of the blood-purchased homage of our hearts. This being the case, can we expect to flourish? Ah! no; the husbandman who gives his time and thoughts to something else during the spring time, shall look in vain for a golden harvest; he shall "reap the whirlwind," as many are now doing.

The opening verses of this chapter furnish a truly terrifying illustration of the inflexible justice and burning jealousy of God; they sound in our ears as with a voice of thunder: "I am a jealous God." Nadab and Abihu, as it were but yesterday, stood before the Lord,—clothed in their garments of glory and beauty, washed in the blood, brought near unto God, made His priests, had passed through all the solemn ceremonies of inauguration into their priestly office. Yes, all this occurred but as yesterday, and to-day they are wasted by the fire of Jehovah, and are seen to fall from their high elevation—a spectacle to men and angels of the fact, that the greater the privilege, the greater the responsibility, and the greater, too, the judgment if that responsibility be not fully met.

What, we may ask, was their sin? Was it murder? Did they stain the curtains of the tabernacle with human blood? Or was it some other abominable sin, from which the moral sense shrinks? No; it was a sin with which the blessed God is grieved by multitudes of professors at this moment—it was *false worship!* "Nadab and Abihu, the sons of Aaron, took either of them his censer and put fire therein, and put incense thereon, and offered strange fire before the Lord, which He commanded them not." "*Strange fire.*" Here was their sin. Here we see men apparently engaged in making preparation for the worship of God; there is the fire, the incense, the censer, and the priest; and, mark, they were not false or spurious priests, but true sons of Aaron, members of the really separated priestly house, clothed in the divinely appointed priestly robes; yet, notwithstanding, *struck dead*, and by whom? by Him whom we call our God and Father! How awfully solemn! Yes, and the fact receives increased solemnity in our view, when we remember that the fire which consumed these false worshippers came from off the "mercy-seat." It was not from mount Sinai's top this fire came, but out "from before the Lord," who was dwelling "between the cherubim above the mercy-seat." God will not be trifled with. Even from the throne of grace will the fire come forth, to lay prostrate those who come before it in any other way than the divinely appointed way. "They died before the Lord!" Dreadful announcement! "Who shall not fear thee, O Lord, and glorify thy name? for

Thou only art holy: for all nations shall come and worship before Thee; for Thy judgments are made manifest" (Rev. xv. 4).

Let us inquire, then, what the "strange fire" was which brought down such terrific judgment upon those priests; and, in order the more clearly to ascertain this, it is only needful that we turn our attention for a moment to *true* worship and the elements which composed it, in the sixteenth chapter of this book. We find the elements of true worship laid before us in the following words: "And he shall take a censer full of burning coals of fire from off the altar before the Lord, and his hands full of sweet incense beaten small, and bring it within the vail: and he shall put the incense upon the fire before the Lord, that the cloud of the incense may cover the mercy-seat that is upon the testimony, that he die not." (Lev. xvi. 13). Here we see that the elements composing true worship were two, viz. *pure fire* and *pure incense.* It must be *living fire* fresh from the altar of God, where it was perpetually fed by the sacrifice of God's own appointment. The doctrine of this is very apparent. On God's altar is seen, day and night, a fire blazing, expressing, in the view of faith, the inflexible holiness of the Divine nature feeding upon the sacrifice of Christ.

Again, the incense must be *pure,* for "ye shall offer no *strange* incense" (Exod. xxx. 7); *i.e.* it must be such as that God can delight therein, and of His own appointment, not that which is according to our own thoughts, for it was only *pure* incense that could offer a proper material for food to the pure living fire from off the altar. Thus, our worship, to be pure, must possess these two qualities: *Christ* must constitute the material of it, and *the Spirit* alone must kindle the flame. This is true worship. When our souls are really happy in the contemplation of Christ and His precious atonement, led into that contemplation by the Holy Ghost, *then alone* we are able to worship "in spirit and in truth." "While I was musing, the fire kindled." While our souls muse on Jesus, our censer sends up its cloud of acceptable incense over the mercy-seat. "God is a Spirit, and they that worship Him must worship Him in spirit and in truth."

Now, false worship is the very reverse of all this. What is it? It is composed of a variety of elements, fleshly thoughts, animal feelings, worked upon by external things, an imposing ceremonial, sensuous rituals, dim religious light, fine music, pomp and circumstance. These are the elements of false worship, and are opposed to the simple worship of the inner sanctuary, "the live coal, and the pure incense." And in looking at Christendom at this moment, do we not see numerous altars smoking with this impure fire and impure incense? Do we not see the most unholy materials consumed upon many a censer, and the smoke thereof going up as an insult rather than a sweet savour to God? Truly we do, and it is needful for us to look well to the condition of our hearts, lest we be carried away into the self-same evil, for we may rest assured that no one who thus trifles with God will escape with impunity.

Let us now note the effect of this upon Aaron. "Then Moses said unto Aaron, This is it that the Lord spake, saying, I will be sanctified in them that come nigh me, and before all the people I will be glorified. *And Aaron held his peace.*" "I was dumb and opened not my mouth, because *Thou* didst it." Aaron saw the hand of the Lord in the solemn scene before him, and *was still;* not a murmur escapes him; "*it is the Lord,*" and "He will be sanctified in them that approach Him." "God is greatly to be feared in the assembly of His saints, and to be had in reverence of all them that are round about Him." There is something unspeakably grand and awful in this scene; Aaron in solemn silence before the Lord; his two living sons on one side, and his two dead ones on the other. What an example of the inflexible justice of God! The bodies of these two men were, it appears, burned by fire, but their priestly robes were untouched, for their cousins were told by Moses to go near and carry them forth; and "they carried them *in their coats* out of the camp." Here we learn a solemn lesson: we may, by disobedience reduce ourselves to such a condition that there will remain nothing but the mere outward form, as seen in the "coats" of Aaron's sons. If any one had looked beneath these coats, he would only have seen the blasted bodies of two priests! The substance, the reality was gone; nought remained but the external covering: such is "a form of godliness without the power," "a name to live while dead."

Lord, keep us very solemn and watchful, for we know but little of our fearful capabilities of evil until we are brought into circumstances to develop them! We may retain the outward appearance of priests, the phraseology of worship, acquaintance with the furniture of God's house, and, after all, be void of godly reality and power in our souls. Oh! reader, let our worship be *pure*, let our hearts be simple as to their object, let us have the *pure* incense and fire, and ever remember that "God is greatly to be feared in the assembly of His saints." I would here observe, that in looking at Aaron and his two sons standing over the dead bodies, we are forcibly reminded of the last chapter of Isaiah, a truly solemn chapter: "They shall go forth, and look upon the carcases of the men that have trangressed against me: for their worm shall not die, neither shall their fire be quenched; and they shall be an abhorring unto all flesh."

But we are now called to contemplate the finest principle of truth in the entire passage. "And Moses said unto Aaron and his sons, Uncover not your heads, neither rend your clothes, lest ye die, and lest wrath come upon all the people; but let your brethren and the whole house of Israel, bewail the burning which the Lord hath kindled And ye shall not go out from the door of the tabernacle, lest ye die; for *the anointing oil of the Lord is upon you.* And they did according to the word of Moses." When one enters upon the office of the priesthood, he is brought out of the region of nature's influence, and must no longer yield to its claims. This is exemplified by Aaron. Natural ties had been burst asunder violently. A melancholy blank had been made in his affections, yet he must not be influenced in the least by all that had taken place before him; and why? "The anointing oil of the Lord was upon him." Surely this is a practical lesson for us. Why has nature such a power over us? Why have earthly circumstances and connections such influence upon us? Why are we so much affected by the things that are passing around us, the vicissitudes of this earthly scene? Why are we so inordinately acted upon by the mere claims and ties of nature? Because we are not *abiding* as we should *in the tabernacle*, with "the anointing oil of the Lord upon us." Here is the real cause of all the failure. In our not realising our priestly place, our priestly dignity, our priestly privileges. Hence it is that we are so carried away by present things, and dragged down from our high elevation as "Kings and priests unto God."

May we then be quickened by this passage, this solemn passage of the Word, to seek more and more of the holy elevation of mind expressed in the words "Uncover not your heads!" May we get more deeply into the mind of God about present things, and our own place therein! God grant it, for the sake of His dear Son!

THE CHURCH.

Ephesians i. 2.

We have in these chapters three distinct points, viz., first, the purpose of God; secondly, the development of that purpose; and, thirdly, the result of that purpose.

It is a thought full of blessedness and comfort to the heart, that it is with God and His deep purposes of grace we have to do, and not with human circumstances. Faith apprehends this; it looks away from what the professing Church has made of herself, and only contemplates what the Church is as the body of Christ—beloved of God, washed in the blood, indwelt by the Holy Ghost. Faith travels backward to eternity, reposes upon the purpose of God, and thus gives the soul power to act amid the most depressing and humiliating circumstances. It was this truth that sustained the spirit of the apostle Paul, while he lay a prisoner at Rome, deserted and despised. He knew that nothing could shake the reality of the purpose of God. Hence he writes: "Blessed be the God and Father of our Lord Jesus Christ, who hath blessed us with all spiritual blessings in heavenly places in Christ: according as He hath chosen us in Him *before the foundation of the world*, that we should be *holy* and *without blame* before Him in love." Here was faith's resting-place. "All spiritual blessings *in the heavenlies*." There was nothing here—all was above. Looking at earth, all might present an aspect of hopeless ruin; but faith ever occupies itself with God's reality; it looks at the Church according to God's predestination, and acts accordingly. If this be not the habit of our souls, we shall have no power at all to get on. If we look at things around us, unbelief at once enters in, with all its reasonings, and renders us powerless; or it may lead us, with uninstructed zeal, to build up the Church after a human model, or to lend our aid to such attempts, which must issue in thorough confusion.

Now, the ever blessed God purposed to have the Church "holy and without blame before Him in love." This was His purpose; and it is just as we are able to get up to God's point of view that we see the Church to be that holy, blameless, lovely thing which God has made her to be in Christ. One of old, who looked at Israel "*in the vision of the Almighty*," was constrained to say, "He hath not beheld iniquity in Jacob, neither hath He seen perverseness in Israel." This is truly precious for the soul. It is not that "iniquity and perverseness" are not there. No; but God does not see them, because He has set the cleansing efficacy of the blood of His own dear Son between Him and all the blots and stains that might trouble the conscience. In the vision of man, who looks only at the outward appearance, the camp of old, or the Church now, might exhibit but a poor spectacle; but in "the vision of the Almighty" it is totally different. The Church is "*all fair*" in the eye of God; and, surely, this is enough.

"Beholders many faults may find,
But they can guess at Jesus' mind,
Content if written in His book."

Yes, truly, content if written in His book; and are we not so? Yea, are we not engraved on His hands, and borne upon His heart continually? Thank God, it is even so. God views the Church as He views Jesus. She is "accepted in the Be loved." "As He is, so are we." "We are in Him that is true." "We are members of His body, of His flesh, and of His bones." "Thou hast loved them as Thou hast loved me." And all this was arranged in the infinite mind of God, before the foundation of the world, before the entrance of sin, before a single member of the Church had breathed the breath of life. "In Thy book (as perhaps we may be allowed to apply a well-known Scripture) were all my members written, which in continuance were fashioned when as yet there was none of them" (Ps. cxxxix). Thus should we view the Church—thus should we think of and act toward her. We must rise to the everlasting counsel of

God concerning her, in order to receive power to serve her perseveringly. If we get off this high ground we must fail altogether. It is impossible for any one to serve the Church, who is not walking in communion with God's thoughts about her. We may make efforts after personal holiness; we may make progress in grace and knowledge; but if these things are not connected with the Church, they are merely selfish efforts. We should increase in holiness of character; we should make progress in grace and knowledge; but these things should ever be connected with the true interests of the Church of Christ; they would then be in harmony with the mind of Him who could say, "The zeal of Thine house hath eaten me up."

Now, this purpose of God was developed in Christ, who is the risen Head of the Church: in Him, too, it finds its accomplishment. All that God purposed concerning the Church was actualized in Christ when He was raised from the dead, and set at the right hand of the majesty in the heavens, and the Holy Ghost was sent down to actualize it in reference to all the members, as it had already been in reference to the Head, to make that true of *them* which was already true of *Him*. This was the object of the mission of the Eternal Spirit. The Son was the standard, the model to which the Church was to be, in process of time, conformed by the operation of the Spirit. "For whom He did foreknow, He also did predestinate to be conformed to the image of His Son, that He might be the first-born among many brethren" (Rom. viii. 29). We have therefore, first, the purpose of God—His own deep and precious thoughts about the Church. We have then the accomplishment of that which was to clear away every obstacle to the full application of that purpose to the Church, viz., the death of Christ, who having taken the Church's place, and made Himself fully answerable for *all* her sins, paid the penalty *for her*, went down into the deepest depths of sorrow for her, cleared away every cloud from the prospect; and then, being raised from the dead, He took His seat at the right hand of God, and sent down the Holy Ghost to form the Church, to bring it into the unity which belonged to it as the body of Christ.

Now, seeing that all that was needed for the application of the purpose of God to the Church, was accomplished in the death and resurrection of Christ, it is impossible that anything can finally prevent its being actualized in reference to all the foreknown and predestined members of the Church. Neither Satan, nor the world, nor sin, nor death, nor aught else, can by any means countervail the purpose of God. Hence the apostle prays for the Ephesians, "that ye may know what is the hope of His calling, what the riches of the glory of His inheritance in the saints, and *what is the exceeding greatness of His power to usward who believe, according to the working of His mighty power* which He wrought in Christ when He raised Him from the dead, and set Him at His own right hand in the heavenly places, far above all principality, and power, and might, and dominion, and every name that is named, not only in this world, but also in that which is to come; and hath put all things under His feet, and gave Him to be the head over all things to the Church, which is His body, the fulness of Him that filleth all in all."

To have this prayer answered in our experience, is to be raised above the influence of every doubtful thought. It seems as if the Holy Ghost would provide a powerful remedy for any hesitating thought that might assault us, while viewing the wondrous counsel of God's will about the Church, and the high and holy destinies marked our for her in the ages to come.

The very position which the prayer occupies is remarkable. The apostle had been dealing with the question of what the Church is in the purpose of God, and he was about to treat of the Church's condition by nature; and the distance between these two points was so vast, that we need to have the eyes of our understanding enlightened in order to know "the exceeding greatness of the power" which could raise us from one to the other. For what is our condition by nature? "Dead in trespasses and sins"—"walking according to the course of this world"—"children of wrath." Such is our state by nature, and not of us Gentiles only, but of the favoured Jews too; and when we look from this state up to the wondrous height of glory which the counsel of God has fixed as the future portion of the Church, we may well pray to have the eyes of our understanding enlightened, that we may know the greatness of God's power to usward. Now, this power "to usward" is the very same power that was brought to bear on Christ when He lay in the grave, beneath the terrible weight of the Church's sin. Christ took the place of greatest distance from God, inasmuch as He was "*made sin.*" He had a weight of sin upon Him which no mortal could bear. Hence, when we behold Him raised to the right hand of God, "far above all principality and power, and every name that is named, not only in this world, but also in that which is to come," we see, at once, the measure of the Church's acceptance. The Church is the body of Christ, His fulness, and, therefore, can never be viewed apart from Him. Hence, if it be asked, How was Jesus raised up from beneath the weight of sin which He had taken upon Himself? the answer is, By the working of *God's mighty power.*

What an expression! The mighty power of God! Who or what could resist it? There was nothing to resist it; it was exercised in most perfect harmony with wisdom, prudence, justice, and truth. The law of God had been magnified and made honourable by the spotless life of the Lord Jesus; all the claims of justice had been satisfied by His death as the spotless Lamb of God; hence "the working of God's mighty power" (*ἐνέργειαν τοῦ κράτους τῆς ἰσχύος*) was brought to bear, and Christ was raised from the dead and set far above all the power of the enemy; and now He can set His foot upon everything that could stand in the way of the Church's full blessedness. He entered into the strong man's house, and took from him his armour wherein he trusted, and spoiled his house, and all this, be it observed, as Head of the Church, and on her behalf.

Now, all this truth about Christ and the Church was shadowed forth in Adam and Eve. In Genesis i. 26, we have the counsel of God respecting man, in the following words: "And God said, Let us make man in our image, after our likeness; and let *them* have dominion over the fish of the sea, and over the fowl of the air, and over the cattle, and over all the earth," &c. Again: "God blessed *them*, and God said unto *them*," &c. It is important, in connection with our subject, to see that, in these verses, we have the counsel of God about Adam and Eve rather than the actual accomplishment of facts. This will appear from the following chapter, where we find the Lord God saying, "It is not good that the man should be *alone*." The purpose of God had not been actualized in reference to Eve when the Divine benediction was pronounced on her in the person of Adam; she was blessed in him—in him, too, she got dominion; she had nothing of, in, nor through herself; ALL WAS IN THE MAN. This is a sublime and glorious truth. The Church is *bound up* in the same "bundle of life" with the Lord Jesus; yea, and in the same bundle of glory likewise. The hand that would wrest from her her portion of life and glory, must wrest it from Him first, for she holds ALL IN HIM.

Here is faith's Divine resting-place; here, too, the standard by which it estimates the Church's place and character. Why should not the Church be pronounced "very good," when looked at in the Person of Christ? Why should not she be blessed, when blessed in Him? When the Church shall shine in all the brightness of the glory of Christ, and share in the honours of His throne, what will it be but the accomplishment of God's blessed purpose about her? Eve was thought of and spoken of before she had been called into being; it was "*them*" (Gen. i.), while none but the man existed. And so surely as Eve was thought of, so surely would she be called into being —but how? "The Lord God caused *a deep sleep* to fall upon Adam, and he slept: and He took *one of his ribs*, and closed up the flesh instead thereof; and the rib which the Lord God had taken from man, made (margin *builded*) He a woman, and brought her unto the man" (Gen. ii. 21, 22).*

* It is interesting to observe that the word used by the LXX. in verse 22, is substantially the same as that which occurs with a preposition referring to the union of Jewish and Gentile believers in Ephesians ii. 22. In the former it is ᾠκοδόμησεν, and in the latter it is συνοικοδομεῖσθε. Indeed, the analogy between Genesis i. and ii. and Ephesians i. and ii., as bearing upon our immediate subject, can hardly fail to

Thus it was that the purpose of God was applied to Eve. Adam had to sleep, and lose a rib, ere the woman could be formed according to the Divine counsel. Just so is it as regards the antitype of all this. The second man, the Lord from heaven, had to descend into the lower parts of the earth, according to the eternal purpose of the Father, ere the Church could enter into the actual enjoyment of the glory and dominion of which we have been constituted joint-heirs with Christ; and it is the aim of the Holy Ghost, in His present work in the Church, to lead every foreknown and predestinated member of the body into the realization of the purpose of God concerning the whole. This attaches special importance to the preaching of the Gospel in all its completeness, "the mystery of the Gospel," as it is called in Ephesians vi.; it being the great instrument by which souls are brought into the Church. The intelligent evangelist will ever keep Christ and the Church in view; he does not preach to swell the ranks of a party, but to gather souls to Christ, in the unity of the body on earth. His object is not only the salvation of sinners, but to have realized and expressed *here* in the believers what is already true and real above—that for which Christ died (John

arrest the spiritual mind. Adam and Eve point to Christ and the Church; Adam's sleep, to Christ's death; and the building of the woman, to the building of the Church by the present operation of the Holy Ghost sent down from heaven. Other minuter analogies might easily be added.

x. 11) and the Spirit came down (Acts i. 2, and 1 Cor. vi. 12). Faith has to do with God's realities.

And now, as to the result of the purposes of God about the Church, what is it? The object which God had in view—simply that. The result *must* correspond with the Divine purpose, for God cannot be frustrated. And what was that object? "That in the dispensation of the fulness of times, He might gather together *in one* all things in Christ." This is the purpose, and this, too, will be the result.* But there is a present result, of which we read in the last verse of chapter ii., viz., "In whom *ye also are builded together* for an habitation of God through the Spirit." God dwells in the Church, not only in the Church (or the assembly of God) as a whole, but in each local assembly *which owns the name of Jesus as the only centre of union, and the Holy Ghost as the only source and power of ministry in the unity of the Church, Christ's body, on earth.* Where these truths are held in power, there is a distinct expression of the present result of God's purpose about the Church:

* ["It is worthy of note that in Ephesians, which contemplates us as already seated in heavenly places in Christ, there is no direct reference to the Lord's coming. So in the kindred epistle to the Colossians; it is not His coming from heaven to them who were on earth (which would involve the thought of distance and separateness, instead of the Head and His body); it is not His coming for us, but our appearing with Him in glory. This is, to my mind, a singularly beautiful sample of the harmony of truth that pervades the Scriptures."]

I pray the reader to pause here, and see if he understands this. It is of real moment that every Christian should prayerfully and solemnly consider the question of what the Church really is; and in doing so, the word of God must be our only guide. We cannot commit ourselves to man on this great question. The Lord alone can teach us to profit. Neither can we view it in the light of circumstances. What power of action can be had by looking at men or things? None whatever. We need what God has given us, a spirit of love and of power and of a sound mind. Led of the Holy Ghost, and subject to Scripture, we shall not long want a clear, calm, and settled conviction of what the Church is, as presented in the New Testament, and learnt in the secret of the Lord's own presence. When, through grace, my reader has gotten this, he will be no more "tossed to and fro, and carried about with every wind of doctrine, by the sleight of men, and cunning craftiness, whereby they lie in wait to deceive; but, speaking the truth in love, he will grow up into Him in all things, which is the head, even Christ." Let us learn from the Lord what His Church is, and then we shall be able, *as we shall feel ourselves bound*, to turn away from everything which is not like it; for conduct should ever be according to conviction. So also we shall seek grace from day to day, to carry out in our respective spheres, and according to our measure of faith, understanding, and power, the Divine purpose about the Church.

Let us take up, for instance, the epistle to the Ephesians, and study it with a teachable and impartial mind, and we shall soon see what the Church *is*: mark, not merely what the Church *is to be*, but what *the Church is now*.

Could one who was divinely taught the doctrine of the Church—could one who knew and valued the place of the Bride, the Lamb's wife, have a happy heart and a peaceful conscience in sanctioning the harlot which commits fornication with the kings of the earth, or with any human imitation of the Church, whereby the Holy Ghost is hindered, dishonoured, and grieved? A religious institution is not necessarily the Church of God; on the contrary, it may be hostile to the Church—a positive barrier to the expression of the unity of the Spirit. Hence, if we will be the upholders of Babylon, we must abandon the idea of holily serving the Church of God, for the two are incompatible. The reader would therefore do well to ponder the fearful consequences of occupying a position hostile to the true interests of Christ's body on earth. True, it will ever be difficult to flesh and blood to live for Christ and the Church, but then it is well worth encountering all the difficulty. The Lord has special joy and complacency in those who sacrifice themselves for the sake of the Church. It was what He did Himself, and all who are filled with His Spirit will follow His example. One who, perhaps, came nearer than any to his Master, could say, "I would that ye knew what great conflict I have for you, and for them at Laodicea, and for as many as have not seen my face in the flesh." And again: "Who now rejoice in my sufferings for you, and fill up that which is behind of the afflictions of Christ in my flesh for His body's sake, which is the Church." Indeed, it was for the purpose of furthering the interests of the Church that Paul desired to remain on earth. "To abide in the flesh," he writes, "is more needful for you. And having this confidence, I know that I shall abide and continue with you all for your furtherance and joy of faith." To him the world presented one vast desert—the scene of his trial and conflict; but when he thought of the beloved Church, he could willingly sacrifice his own feelings to further its joy. Blessed servant! Would that we had more of his spirit. Wherever Paul went, the Church was his object; when he preached, he preached for the Church; when he made tents, it was for the Church likewise. *He lived for Christ and the Church;* and, oh! my reader, if you and I love the name of Jesus, ought we not to live for the same object? Do not say, What can *I* do for the Church? You can do much, very much for it; you can, by precept, and, above all, by example, promote its unity; you can bear testimony against everything that would hinder that unity. First, ascertain what the Church is, so that you may not be calling that the Church which is nothing more than a human arrangement, set up for the professed purpose of providing for the religious wants of men, whether Christians or not. Could such a thing be the Church? And if it be not the Church, it must be opposed to it, and subversive of its blessing and testimony on earth. For if we gather not with Christ, we can but scatter. Again, you should beware of upholding anything which practically denies the unity of the Church, by setting up any other centre of union than the name of Jesus.

The body of Christ on earth consists of all who, savingly believing in His name, are indwelt by the Holy Ghost. As such, they will endeavour to "walk worthy of the vocation wherewith they are called," and "to keep the unity of the Spirit in the bond of peace." It may be well just to add a word here as to the strict meaning of the term "the Church," Christ's body, as used in the epistle to the Ephesians, etc. And be it noted well, that the apostle here is not treating of an invisible unity in heaven, but of the Church on earth. Let any spiritual person read Ephesians iv., and answer if the body, the members, the gifts there treated of, are in heaven or on earth. (Compare also 1 Cor. xii. and Rom. xii.) Are these apostles, prophets, teachers, healings, for the Church in heaven? And, if not in heaven, where, if not in the Church here below? Unquestionably the Church will still enjoy a special place of nearness to the Lord as His body in heaven. But the Scriptures say little of a truth so obvious and almost self-evident, while they speak much and frequently of the Church as one body on earth. We learn from these and other portions of the Word of God, that the Church of God did not begin to be formed here below until the ascension of Christ to the right hand of God, and the consequent descent of the Holy Ghost. After these things had become accomplished facts, believers began to be brought into a position different from, and higher than, anything that had yet been known. Believers, previously, did not form a part of this body, for it was *when the second Adam slept* that His Eve was formed. God, in His manifold wisdom, has various spheres of blessing, various departments of service and worship for His people. There are the heavenlies and the earthlies. The Spirit speaks of "every family" (*πᾶσα πατριὰ*) in heaven and on earth. These things are not to be confounded. "The glory of the celestial is one, and the glory of the terrestrial is another."

Is it, therefore, asked, what is the precise period to which the formation of the Church is confined? The answer is very simple, viz.; From the time that Christ took His seat at the right hand of God, and sent the Holy Ghost from on high to baptize believers into one body, until the time when He shall leave it to meet His Church in the air. (Compare Ps. cx. 1, and 1 Thess. iv. 14–17.) This, be it long or short, is, properly speaking, the Church period. It must be confined to this; for, before its commencement, and after its expiration, *the earthly family*, the seed of Abraham, must be regarded as the special object of the Divine dealings on earth. This, then, makes the matter very simple. It requires no effort to understand the peculiarly unique and heavenly character of the Church of Christ. The time during which the Church of God is being formed is just while Christ, the risen and glorified Head, is hidden in the heavens, and while the earth ceases to be the scene of God's manifested operations. Neither the earth nor any particular land is publicly owned of God now; it was once, before the Church period commenced, and it will be again after that period has ceased. But *now*, God is gathering out of the earth the heavenly family to be the body of Christ, His Bride—to be conformed to Him in everything, to be as separated from the world as He is, to have nothing on earth, either in the way of standing, hope, or calling.

But, it may be asked, Were not Abel, Abraham, Moses, and David, members of the Church? The answer to this is fully involved in what has been already advanced. If the formation of the Church must be confined to the precise period above named (and is it not?) then those who lived a thousand years, more or less, before that period commenced, cannot be regarded as part of it. They belonged to some of the families referred to in Ephesians iii. 15 (which does not merge all in one family, but is rightly rendered, "*every family* in heaven and on earth is named"), but they do not belong to the Church, properly so called. They were saved by faith in Christ, no doubt, and they will occupy, in the ages to come, a place suited to them in the manifold wisdom of God; but we must not unduly limit nor extend the actings of the blessed God; He will order the various departments of His happy house according to His own grace and wisdom, and not according to our foolish thoughts. Scripture applies the term, the Church of God, of the first-born, etc., to the saints between Pentecost and the Lord's coming again, and to none others. If it do, nothing can be more easy of proof. Let a single text be produced which speaks of the saints before and after those termini as the Church of God, or body of Christ. But there is none. And the only safe course is to give up our own thoughts and to follow the unerring Word. Nor is it merely the name which is peculiar; but there are special privileges and a special walk, which are connected, so far as Scripture speaks, with the believers who are found in the Church period, and with none else. And to me it is clear, that if you make the Church to be the aggregate of all saints from the beginning to the end of all things, you lose entirely the power of the truth of its union as a proper living body on earth, indwelt of the Holy Ghost, and made one spirit with the Lord in heaven.

The Lord give us to know more and more of His own mind concerning us, that we may serve Him more intelligently and devotedly!

THE PASSOVER IN EGYPT.

Exodus xii.

The Passover celebrated in Egypt is the well-known type of Christ averting from His people the judgment which overtakes the ungodly. The destroying angel passed through the land of Egypt, and smote the first-born in every house. Israel escaped by the death of the lamb, and by that alone. The blood sprinkled on the door-post told the destroyer that the sentence of death had been already executed, and he therefore passed over. Hence, then, the blood distinguished the houses of the Israelites from those of the Egyptians. This was the grand distinction. When it was a question of life or death, the blood, and the blood *alone*, fixed the line of demarcation: "When *I* see *the blood*, I will pass over." This was God's record, presented for the obedience of faith. The blood was outside, and Israel were inside; and hence they could not see the blood; nor was that needful. All that was needed was simple faith in God's record; and the more simple the faith, the fuller was their peace. It was their privilege to eat the lamb, within their houses, with tranquillized hearts, while the destroyer passed through with unsheathed sword, inflicting terrible judgment on all who were not sheltered beneath the blood.

How simple is this! How striking! How much we learn from it! Throughout the vast mass of profession around us, there are two classes; those who have received God's salvation, in the accomplished work of Christ, and those who, rejecting Him, build upon the multiplied forms of false or defective religion with which Christendom abounds. God's way of salvation is simple—as simple as it is complete: "If thou shalt confess with thy mouth the Lord Jesus, and shalt believe in thine heart that God hath raised Him from the dead, thou shalt be saved" (Rom. x. 9). Christ is God's salvation; and, moreover, it is God's estimate of Christ that forms the basis of the believer's peace. It is very necessary to understand distinctly this latter point. There are many who suffer not a little by looking at their faith, instead of at the Object of faith; in fact, by unwittingly making a kind of saviour of their faith. Now, faith is only the hand, as it were, that takes hold of the gift of God, just as the hand of a hungry man takes the proffered bread, and conveys it to his mouth. If I have my eye off Christ, and begin to examine the amount of my faith, I must of necessity decline, for He is the *only one* on whom the sinner's eye can rest. Genuine faith never looks at itself, but only at Jesus. A faithful Israelite would not have thought of going out to look at the lintel of his door, nor yet of examining the amount of his faith. No; he simply rested in the fact put before him in those precious words, "When I see the blood, I will pass over." It was not said, "When I see your girded loins, your shod feet, your unleavened bread, I will pass over." These things were most needful, yea, essential, but not to save from the sword of the destroyer. To meet this, nothing could avail but the blood of the lamb.

It is well that my reader should be clear as to the distinction between the ground of peace, and that which is the spring of holiness and devotedness in his daily course; in other words, that he should understand the distinction between the work of Christ *for* us, and the work of the Spirit *in* us. The former is illustrated by the blood on the lintel without: the latter, by the Israelites' actings within. When any one, through grace, receives Christ, in the Divine efficacy of His accomplished work, he is introduced into a position in which God can address him as to his conduct; he becomes the subject of parental care and discipline. But then he must be careful not to confound the question of his walk with the ground of his perfect, his profound peace in the presence of God.

Many, I feel persuaded, suffer in this way; they do not understand the fulness of Christ for them, and their everlasting completeness in Him, together with the settled judgment of God about them. Now, while there is any dimness or uncertainty as to this there can neither be settled peace of conscience, nor any intelligent ground of Christian activity. Everything will be referred to the question of peace, rather than to the glory of Christ, which should be our aim, and which will be our aim in proportion as we enter into the Divine reality of what we are in Christ, through the infinite grace of God. The more we realize the truth that everything has been accomplished by Christ, for the perfect establishment of our peace in connexion with the holiness of God, the more we shall see how futile is every thought about ourselves. A question as to the believer's peace is, in reality, a question as to the accomplishment of the work of Christ. If you touch one, you touch the other; for "Christ is our peace." He is "the same yesterday, to-day, and for ever."

And not only is He the same always, but God's estimate of Him and of us in Him, is also the same—"Ye are complete in Him who is the head of all principality and power." "As He is, so are we in this world." "Wherein He hath made us accepted in the Beloved." "He hath not beheld iniquity in Jacob, neither hath He seen perverseness in Israel" (Num. xxiii. 21). Not that iniquity and perverseness are not there; for "if we say that we have no sin, we deceive ourselves, and the truth is not in us." It would not give us any peace to be told that the Lord's people have not perverseness in them; but that *He hath not beheld it* tranquillizes the heart most blessedly. It is God's grace that blots out sin, through the precious blood of Jesus. He delights to do this; yea, it is His glory. "Thou hast cast *all* my sins behind Thy back."

This, beloved Christian reader, should banish every fear from your heart. God is not looking at your sin, but at the blood of the Lamb; and in that He sees the exquisite fruit of His own love, and triumphs in it. Now, if God is not looking at your sin, why should you keep dwelling upon it? If He graciously triumphs in the fruit of His love, why should you not triumph in it also? The spring of your communion is your keeping your eye fixed upon the same object that God is looking at. Now, if God is looking at Christ, and you are looking at your sins, of necessity there can be no communion. "Can two walk together except they be agreed?" God says, by virtue of the blood of Christ, "Your sins and your iniquities will I remember no more." Are you calling them to remembrance? How many are anxiously occupied about the question of personal peace, which really stands at the very threshold of the Christian course! This sorrowful state of soul may arise from various causes. It may arise from imperfect or muddy views of the gospel; from not seeing the fulness of Christ, and the absolutely settled character of the forgiveness of sins.

But there is another cause, and one of a far more grave and serious nature: viz., a careless and an unconscientious walk; and cases of this melancholy kind often run to a great extreme—even to actual despair. Such cases teach the importance of seeking a close and faithful walk with God. "He will keep the feet of His saints;" but they are exhorted to "keep their hearts with all diligence." The Spirit reveals Christ, and, if not grieved by sin and worldliness, will build up the soul in His fulness, and establish it in the peace of God, which passeth all understanding. But, alas! when conscience is tampered with—when we sin against light—when we walk in an indolent and a self-indulgent spirit—when we let in the world upon our hearts, then the eye becomes dim, and the understanding darkened; feebleness and langour take the place of energy and vigour; and unless the soul be thoroughly broken down under the sense of its delusion, and restored by the grace of God, in all probability Satan will entangle it in the destructive meshes of carnality and worldliness; or, it may be, will well-nigh drive it into the dread region of infidelity.

Should this paper fall into the hands of any one suffering in this way, let me entreat him at once to pause, and having ascertained, by honest self-judgment, the real cause of his low and heavy state, to bring it into the presence of his heavenly Father, and thus confess, judge, and put away his evil. "If we confess our sins, He is faithful and just to forgive us our sins, and to cleanse us from all unrighteousness."

There is no reason why the believer should continue in a low or impoverished state of soul, unless he is deliberately trifling with conscience, and grieving the Spirit of God. It is his privilege to have Christ, in all His Divine fulness, between his soul and everything, no matter what—sins, infirmities, circumstances; and when the eye is steadily fixed upon, and filled with Christ, nothing can interfere with his peace. But the secret cause of the low condition of so many of God's dear people is, that they have let slip Christ, and allowed other things to come in and occupy their hearts. *He* has been displaced; *they* have lost the freshness of the sense of what He is, and have therefore sunk down into a cold, formal condition. Moreover, the affections, feeling the lack of a definite object around which to entwine themselves, have gone out after the world.

Nothing keeps the heart so free and peaceful as a single eye to Christ. There may be much to try and depress the heart; still there is peace. "In the world ye shall have tribulation, but in me, peace." The Lord Jesus does not promise us exemption from tribulation; no, but He promises us peace *in* tribulation, and this is far more gracious. He came into the midst of His poor, terrified disciples, and said, "*Peace* be unto you." He did not take them *out of* their circumstances, but gave them peace *in* them. This is Divine. The believer should, like the Israelite, sit within, in the blessed fixedness of faith, feeding upon Christ, knowing that the blood of sprinkling is between him and all without. The worst that could come was death and judgment but these had already been executed, and of this the blood on the lintel was the witness. It was impossible that anything could harm those who had taken shelter beneath the blood of the lamb.

It should be remarked, however, that peace of conscience, and peace of heart, are distinct things. Many have the former, who do not enjoy the latter. Settled repose of heart in Christ is a precious fruit of simple communion with Him. It puts an end to all that restless anxiety which so eats up spiritual life. To the heart at rest—fully at rest in Jesus—circumstances are but of small moment. "He shall not be afraid of evil tidings, *his heart* is fixed, trusting in the Lord." It is dishonouring to the Lord to see His people giving way to cares and anxieties about present things, and moreover adopting the plans and arrangements current amongst the children of this world. Men say, or at least get abundant reason to say, that there is no difference between Christians and other people, inasmuch as all are seen pursuing the same objects, and pursuing them in the same way. When God's sufficiency fills the soul, plans and arrangements are little thought of. It is really wonderful to perceive how easily the soul loses the practical sense of God's presence and God's sufficiency. It is not that one ceases to be a Christian; this is not at all in question; but, alas! how many Christians are there who do not habitually walk with God! And yet the secret of true victory over nature and the world is, to walk with God. Nature is kept down, and the world is shut out;

but when the soul is withdrawn from its blessed centre in God, everything becomes a difficulty.

We shall now look a little at the circumstances which accompanied the passover. The blood on the lintel, as we have seen, formed the simple basis of the Israelite's security. It was an accomplished fact, with which he had nothing to do, save to repose in its efficacy. But there were other points of deep interest and solemn moment, into which the spiritual mind can enter with much profit.

First, then, *the lamb was eaten "roast with fire."* No other process could have told out the significant principle with the same emphasis. The action of fire upon the body of the lamb gave expression as forcibly as type could do, to the intensity of Christ's sufferings, when he exposed His blessed Person to the full action of Jehovah's righteous wrath against sin. Now, it was one thing to rest in the security of the shed blood *without*, and another thing to eat of the "lamb roast with fire." Hence, the apostle says, "that I may know Him, and the power of His resurrection, and *the fellowship of his sufferings.*" Here was the desire of one who had already rested in the blood of sprinkling. The fellowship of Christ's sufferings is but little known even by those who are resting in the precious efficacy of Christ's blood; were it more entered into, there would be far more depth of experience and power of Christian action, than there are. We are too ready to rest content with knowing the value of the blood, without feeding on the Lamb, and thus we lose much of what is really our privilege in the way of personal fellowship with Jesus. We are introduced by the blood into a position in which we can dwell with ever-deepening joy upon the intrinsic excellency of the Person of Christ. It is not merely the work which has been done, but the One who has done it. The former is properly the object for the sinner, the latter for the saint; and the more the saint is enabled to enter into what Christ is, the more perfect will be his repose in his work.

Again, *the lamb was eaten with unleavened bread.* This marked the power of holiness, as the practical result of that nearness to God into which the blood had introduced the soul. But, my reader, observe, this holiness is the result of Christ's work applied to the soul by the power of the Holy Ghost, and does not, in any wise, form the basis of our peace in the presence of God. This should be clearly understood; for the fact is, that this distinction will be found to constitute the great difference between true Christianity and all the false systems of religion of the present day. True Christianity puts Christ as the prominent object before the soul, and, moreover, shows that all real fruit to God must flow from the knowledge of our completeness in Him: false religion, on the other hand, puts Christ in the background—puts Him in the distance, and teaches the sinner that he must work his way upward by virtue of his own fancied holiness. Terrible delusion! Oh! for a simpler, clearer, fuller view of Jesus!

Lastly, *the lamb was eaten with bitter herbs.* This expresses the believer's experience, under the teaching of the Spirit, of the bitterness of that which dwells in him, which, though it has been most fully met in the cross, must ever be recognised as that which brought the Son of God down into the horrible pit and miry clay. It is only in the cross that the real heinousness of sin can be seen; and though it is there viewed in the light of that which puts it away for ever, yet the heart is self-judged and humbled, even while it rests in an accomplished redemption. There is also much precious instruction to be drawn from the mode in which the Israelite was to be habited at the paschal feast. The girded loin expressed readiness for action; the shod foot and staff expressed a pilgrim and dependent spirit.

Let me say, in conclusion, that the highest thought of all is, to have *Christ Himself* before the soul. It will not suffice to have thoughts of His work merely—thoughts of what He has done for *us.* There is much of mere selfishness in all this. We must be drawn to Jesus because of what He is; and this, so far from detracting from the value of His work, will deepen our sense of it every day.

JESUS RISEN.

John xx.

Deep and varied as are the necessities of the soul, they are all met by the death and resurrection of Christ. If it be a question of sin that affects the soul, the resurrection is the glorious proof of the complete putting away of it. The moment I see Jesus at the right hand of God, I see an end of sin; for I know He could not be there if sin was not fully atoned for. "He was delivered for our offences;" He stood as our Representative; He took upon Him our iniquities, and went down into the grave under the weight thereof. "But God raised Him from the dead;" and, by so doing, expressed His full approbation of the work of redemption. Hence we read, "He was raised again for our justification." Resurrection, therefore, meets the need of the soul, as regards the question of sin.

Then, again, when we proceed farther, and enter upon the trying and difficult path of Christian testimony, we find that Jesus risen is a sovereign remedy for all the ills of life. This is happily exemplified for us in John xx. Mary repairs to the sepulchre, early in the morning. And, as we learn from the parallel passage in Mark, her heart was not only sad at the loss of her gracious friend, but also tried by the difficulty of removing the stone from the mouth of the cave. The resurrection removed, at once, her *sorrow* and her *burden*. Jesus risen filled the blank in her desolated affections, and removed from her shoulders the load which she was unable to sustain. She found the stone rolled away from the sepulchre, and she found also her beloved Lord, whom death had for a season snatched from her view. Such mighty things could resurrection accomplish on behalf of a poor needy mortal.

Nor is it otherwise with us now. Have our hearts been broken and bereaved by the stern, rude hand of death? Has his cold breath chilled our affections? What is the remedy? Resurrection. Yes; resurrection, that great restorer, not merely of "tired" but of ruined nature, fills up all blanks—repairs all breaches—remedies all ills. If the conscience be affected by a sense of sin, resurrection sets it at rest, by the assurance that the Surety's work has been fully accepted. If the heart be bowed down with sorrow, and torn by the ravages of death, resurrection heals, soothes and binds it up, by securing the restoration and reunion of all who have gone before; it tells us to "sorrow not as others which have no hope, for if we believe that Jesus died, and rose again, even so them also which sleep in Jesus will God bring with Him" (1 Thess. iv. 13, 14). It is commonly thought that time fills up all the blanks which death has made in the affections; but the spiritual mind could never regard time, with its sorrowful vicissitudes, as a substitute for resurrection and its immortal joys. The poor worldling may, perhaps, find, in passing circumstances, something to fill up the void which death makes, but not so the Christian; to him, resurrection is the grand object: to that he looks as the only instrumentality by which all his losses can be retrieved, and all his evils remedied.

So also in the matter of burden and pressure from present circumstances; the only relief is in resurrection. Till then we have but to toil on from day to day, bearing the burden and enduring the travail of the present sorrowful scene. We may, like Mary, feel disposed to cry out, "Who shall roll us away the stone?" Who? The risen Jesus. Apprehend resurrection, and you are raised above the influence of every burden. It is not that we may not have many a burden to carry; no doubt, we may; but our burdens shall not sink us into the dust, because our hearts are buoyed up by the blessed truth that our Head is risen from the dead, and is now seated at the right hand of God, and, moreover, that our place is there with Him. Faith leads the soul upward, even into the holy serenity of the Divine presence—it enables us to cast our burden on the Lord, and to rest assured that He will sustain it for us. How often have we shrunk from the thought of some trial or burden which appeared, in the distance, like a dark cloud upon the horizon, and yet, when we approached it, we "found the stone rolled away from the sepulchre." The risen Jesus had rolled it away. He had removed the dark cloud, and filled up the scene with the light of His own gracious countenance. Mary had come to the sepulchre expecting to find a great stone between her and the object of her affections, but instead of that, she found Jesus risen between her and the dreaded difficulty. She had come to anoint a dead body, but arrived to be blessed and made happy, by a risen Saviour. Such is God's way—such the power and value of resurrection. Sins, sorrows, and burdens all vanish, when we find ourselves in the presence of a living Lord. When John, in the island of Patmos, had fallen to the dust, as one dead, what was it that raised him up? Resurrection—the living Jesus; "I am He that liveth and was dead; and, behold, I am alive for evermore." This set him on his feet. Communion with Him who had wrested life from the very grasp of death, removed his fears and infused divine strength into his soul.

In the case of Peter and John, too, we find another instance of the power of resurrection. In them it is not so much a question of sin, or sorrow, and burden, as of difficulty. Their minds are evidently puzzled by all that met their view at the sepulchre. To see grave-clothes so carefully arranged in the very tomb, was unaccountable. But they are only puzzled, because "as yet, they knew not the scripture that He must rise again from the dead." Nothing but resurrection could solve their difficulty. Had they known that, they would have been at no loss to account for the arrangement of the grave-clothes; they would have known that the Destroyer of death had been there, doing His mighty work, and had left behind Him the traces of His triumph. Such was the meaning of the scene at the tomb; at least it was calculated to teach that lesson. The Lord Jesus had calmly and deliberately passed through the conflict. He had exhibited no haste—no perturbation. He had taken time to set in order His grave-clothes and His tomb; He showed that it required no strained effort on His part to vanquish the power of death. However, Peter and John knew not this; and, therefore, they went away to their own home. The strength of Mary's affection made her linger still; love was more influential than knowledge; and though her heart was breaking, she remained at the sepulchre; she would rather weep near the spot where her Lord was laid, than go anywhere else. But resurrection settled every thing. It filled up the blank in Mary's broken heart, and solved the difficulty in the minds of Peter and John. It dried up *her* tears and put a stop to *their* amazement. Jesus risen is, in good truth, the sovereign remedy for all evils, and nothing is needed but faith to use Him.

At ver. 19, we have a fresh illustration of the principle on which we are dwelling. "Then the same day at evening, being the first day of the week, when *the doors were shut* where the disciples were assembled *for fear of the Jews*, came Jesus and stood in the midst, and said unto them, Peace be unto you." Here the closed door evidenced the fear of the disciples. They were afraid of the Jews. And what could remedy their fear? Nothing but communion with their risen Lord. Nor did He (blessed be His name!) leave them destitute of that remedy; He appeared amongst them—He pronounced His benediction upon them. "Peace be unto you," said He. "Peace," not because their door was secured, but because Jesus was risen. Who could harm them, while they had in heir midst the mighty Vanquisher of death and hell?

There is unspeakable value in this word "peace," used by such an One, at such a time. The peace that flows from fellowship with the risen Son of God cannot be ruffled by the vicissitudes and storms of this world; it is the peace of the inner sanctuary—the peace of God which passeth all understanding. Why are we so much troubled, at times, by the condition of things around us? Why do we betake ourselves, if not to the closed door, at least to some other human resource? Surely, because we are not walking with our eye steadily fixed on Him who was dead, but who is alive for evermore, who has all power in heaven and on earth. Did we but realize that our portion is in Him, yea that He Himself is our portion, we should be far less affected by the prospects of this poor world. The politics, the agriculture, the commerce of earth, would find their proper place in our hearts, if we could remember that "we are dead, and our life is hid with Christ in God." It is commonly said, that while we are here we must take an interest in the circumstances, the prospects, the destinies of earth. But then, "our citizenship is in heaven." We are not of earth at all. Those who are risen with Christ are no longer of earth. All that in us (I mean believers) which could have any affinity with earth—all that which can be called nature, is dead, and should be reckoned as dead, and our life is in heaven, where we are now in spirit and principle. No doubt, if we only see ourselves as earthly men, we shall be occupied with earthly things; but if we see ourselves as heavenly men, we shall, as a consequence, be occupied about heavenly things. "If ye then be risen with Christ, seek *those things which are above.*"

This is simple. "*Things above*" are those which we are commanded to seek, and that because we are "risen with Christ." The difference between Abraham, in his day, and a believer now, may be thus stated: Abraham was going from earth to heaven; the believer has come from heaven to earth; *i. e.* in spirit, and by faith. Abraham was a pilgrim on earth, because *he sought* a heavenly country; the believer is a pilgrim on earth, because *he has gotten* a heavenly country. The Christian should regard himself as one who has come from heaven, to go through the scenes and engagements of earth. This would impart a high and heavenly tone to his character and walk here. The Lord grant that it may be more so with all who name the name of Jesus!

It may be remarked, in conclusion, that the Lord Jesus remedied the fear of His poor disciples by coming into their midst, and associating Himself with them in all their circumstances. It was not so much a question of actual deliverance from the matter that caused the fear, but rather raising their souls above it by fellowship with Himself. They forgot the Jews, they forgot their fear, they forgot everything, because their souls were occupied with their risen Lord. The Lord's way is often to leave His people in trial and to be with them therein. Paul might desire to get rid of the thorn, but the answer was, "My grace is sufficient for thee." It is a far richer mercy to have the grace and presence of Jesus *in* the trial, than to be delivered *from* it. The Lord allowed Shadrach, Meshach, and Abednego to be cast into the furnace; but, if He did, He came down and walked with them therein. This was infinitely more gracious of Him, and more honourable to them, than if He had interposed on their behalf before they were cast in.

May it be our heart's desire to find ourselves in company with the risen Lord, as we pass through this trying scene, and then, whether it be the furnace of affliction, or the storm of persecution, we shall have peace; whether it be the bereavement of the heart, the burden of the shoulder, the difficulty of the mind, the fear or unbelief of the heart, all will be remedied by fellowship with Him who was raised from the dead.

INSIDE THE VEIL, OUTSIDE THE CAMP.

Hebrews x. 9–16.

THE power of our path—of our walk in this world, is the understanding, through the Holy Ghost, of our identification with Christ in all our ways, and our being set in the world to manifest Him, not merely to know that we have salvation, and the purging of our consciences through His most precious blood. The testimony of a Christian bears this character, he is treading in the footsteps of Christ. "To me, to live is Christ:" again, "I am crucified with Christ: nevertheless I live; yet not I, but Christ liveth in me: and the life which I now live in the flesh I live by the faith of the Son of God, who loved me, and gave Himself for me"—(faith not *in* but "*of* the Son of God," that is, the same faith by which Jesus walked up and down in the world, is the faith by which we are called to live.) That puts each of us in the place of responsibility as to our ways, our habits, our feelings, and objects. Are we realizing the responsibility of living Christ? That is really what the Church of God is set in the world for—to be the expression of Christ in His absence. A Christian's conscience often satisfies itself with handing to the unconverted man the Bible, so that he may read what Christ was; but this is not the object for which Christ has left us here.—"*Ye* are the epistles of Christ, known and read of all men." Are we such an epistle as persons can read? It is not a person's coming to me, and saying, What is your creed? What views do you hold? and the like. If I am not an expression of the ways and feelings of Christ, I am a stumbling-block, rather than otherwise. The Christian should be the living, breathing expression of Christ—of the principles, features, graces, of the character of Christ. Alas! the whole of Christianity is often made to consist in a set of opinions: one gets his place and is characterized by what opinions he holds. We are called upon necessarily to live the Christ in whom we believe; we are one with Him, and are called to show forth what He is. But the whole power, by which I am to act and to show that, is the understanding that I am one with Him.

There are two great stages of Christ's path, and of the believer's, as identified with Him, presented to us in the Epistle to the Hebrews. The first ends (chapter x.) where the soul is set in "the holies." Up to that the Holy Ghost is conducting us along, step by step; there He sets us down in this blessed place, "having boldness to enter into the holiest, by the blood of Jesus, by a new and living way, which He hath consecrated for us, through the veil, that is to say, His flesh."

The power of intelligent devotedness is the understanding of the perfect purging of our consciences. Many do not understand this; they are aiming at getting it, and that is a complete reversing of God's order. I have a purged conscience; I go on, not to obtain it, but because I have it. How do I get it? Not by anything that I have done, by my frames or feelings, as a matter of attainment or experience; the Holy Ghost teaches us that it is by the blood of Jesus.

He shows the glory of the person of Christ, as contrasted with angels and with Moses; that of His priesthood as contrasted with Aaron's; that of His sacrifice, as contrasted with the sacrifices under the law. And what is the result? We have a purged conscience. He has set us down *within the veil.* It is not what one Christian has, and what another is struggling after, but the common platform of all—we *all* have a purged conscience. Some suppose that the blood of Christ has put away our sins before conversion; and then, as to what becomes of those after, they are met by the priesthood of Christ; but this is not what He says: it is by the blood of Christ; we are within the holiest with a perfectly-purged conscience, with "no more conscience of sins." It is just worthy of the sacrifice of Christ to put me in possession of this, and nothing short of it; *all* my sins, not some of them, blotted out. There, where the

High Priest could go in once every year, and only then, the simplest believer is set down.

When one comes to deal closely with souls, one discovers what doubts, clouds, fears, and anxieties, have possession of and distress them. If the blood of Christ does anything for us, it sets us there without spot, or wrinkle, or any such thing. "Having, therefore, brethren, boldness to enter into the holiest by the blood of Jesus . . . . let us draw near," etc. There is no difference here between apostle and others; the apostle Paul and the thief on the cross: in other words, all alike have a common place within the veil.

The priesthood of Christ comes in to maintain me practically where the blood of Christ has set me. As in the expression in the Epistle of John, "If any man sin, we have an advocate with the Father, Jesus Christ the righteous [Jesus Christ is at God's right hand on all principles of righteousness], and He is the propitiation [the mercy-seat] for our sins." We are never told, in the New Testament, that we are to *ask* for the pardon of sins, there is not such an expression as this. "If we confess our sins, He is faithful and just to forgive us our sins, and to cleanse us from all unrighteousness." Nor is this distinction unimportant. It is a much easier thing for a child to ask for pardon for some fault than to confess it. We may be asking for pardon for any special sin, and we have no Scripture warrant to know that it is put away; but when we confess it, it is a matter of *faith* to know that it is put away. I am speaking now of a believer: were it the question of an unconverted person, the blood of Christ meets that. God is "faithful and just (not gracious and merciful merely), to forgive us our sins," etc. The moment I have judged myself about it, I am entitled to know that it is gone.

What a very wondrous place to set the believer in at the very outset of his course of discipleship!—washed from his sins, his conscience purged, set down in the unclouded sense of the light of God's own countenance! But what to do? to rest there? No; that is the foundation on which the superstructure of practical devotedness is based. Legalism and antinomianism are alike met. What does the system of legalism say? You must work yourself up into this place of acceptance. The gospel says, Christ has put me there. I never could get there; the law has proved that. When God gave the law, what was He doing? "You shall do this," "You shall not do that," brought out what man's heart was; it was impossible he could do what God was telling him he ought to do, and impossible he should not be what God was telling him not to be:—"As many as are of the works of the law are under the curse." I can never, by works of law, get into the holiest of all. I am put there as the result of what Christ has accomplished for me on the cross; and this is stated at the very outset of the epistle: "When He had by Himself purged our sins, He sat down on the right hand of the Majesty on high" (chap. i. 3). Why does it say "sat down"? To evidence the completion of the work. Aaron never sat down; there was no seat prepared for the priest, either in the tabernacle or the temple.

What does antinomianism lead men to say? "I have it, I possess it all in Christ," and there it ends. But no! the gospel puts me there, to run the blessed race that is set before me, in ardent, earnest breathing of the soul to become like Christ.

If the first division sets me down *within the holiest*, the second places me *without the camp*. I find Christ, as it regards my conscience, "inside the veil." I find Christ, as it regards my heart, "outside the camp."

It does not become us to take only the comfort which flows from our knowing Christ to be within the veil—the comfort His sacrifice gives us, I must seek practical identification with Him outside the camp. Christ within the veil tranquillizes my conscience. Christ outside the camp quickens, energizes my soul to run more devotedly the race set before me. "The bodies of those beasts, whose blood is brought *into the sanctuary* by the high priest for sin, are burned without the camp. Wherefore Jesus also, that He might sanctify the people with His own blood, suffered without the gate. Let us go forth, therefore, *unto Him without the camp*, bearing His reproach" (ver. 11–13). No two points are morally more remote than *inside the veil* and *outside the camp*, and yet they are brought together here. Inside the veil was the place where the shekinah of God's glory dwelt; outside the camp the place where the sin-offering was burned—no place gives such an idea of distance from God as that. It is blessed to know that the Holy Ghost presents to me Jesus filling up all that is between these two points. I have nothing to do whatever with the camp. The camp was the place of ostensible profession (in type, the camp of Israel; in antitype, the city of Jerusalem). Why did Christ suffer without the gate? In order to show the setting aside of the mere machinery of Israel's outward profession.

We may be clear as to the work of Christ being done for us (and God forbid there should be a cloud cast across the blessedness of that), knowing the conscience to be made perfect; but is tranquility of conscience all I want? is there no responsibility? is Christ's voice from within the veil all? has He no voice outside the camp? It will be found that, after all, the joy, peace, liberty, flowing from our hearing Christ's voice inside the veil, is very much dependent on our listening to His voice outside the camp. Those who know most of suffering with Him, and bearing His reproach, will know most of the blessedness of His place within the veil. Our conduct, our ways, our path through the earth, must be tested by Christ.—"Would Christ be there? would Christ do this?" The Holy Ghost must be grieved if the saint pursues a course contrary to that which

Christ would have pursued; and then the soul must be lean. How can a grieved Spirit testify of Christ—how can He give the soul comfort and joy and peace of His testimony to Him? How can I be enjoying Christ if I am not walking in company with Him? We know that we cannot enjoy the company of a person unless we are where that person is—where then is Christ? "Outside the camp."—"Let us go forth, therefore, unto *Him* without the camp, bearing *His* reproach." This is not to go forth to men, or to opinions, to a church, or to a creed, but to Christ Himself. We are not of the world—why? Because Christ is not of the world; the measure of our separation from the world is the measure of Christ's separation. "For here have we no continuing city;" do our hearts seek one?—some set of circumstances or the like, a something, on which to lean? Are we saying, as it were, "Oh do leave me something"? like Lot pleading for Zoar, "Is it not a little one?" do not take it all away, "is it not a little one; and my soul shall live!" Lot's was a heart going out after a little of the world still. When the heart is filled with Christ it can give up the world, there is no difficulty in doing it then. The mere saying, "Give up this," or "give up that," to one loving the world, will be of no avail; what I have to do is to seek to minister to that soul more of Christ.

I am outside the camp, I am seeking a city that is to come, I am waiting for Him who is to come.

In this condition, of dislodgement from the world and from its system, I find myself in two positions —one towards God, and the other towards man. The first, " By Him, therefore, let us offer the sacrifices of praise to God continually, that is, the fruit of our lips, giving thanks to His name" (ver. 15). The second, the lovely development of the spirit of active benevolence of the next verse, " But to do good and to communicate forget not; for with such sacrifices God is well pleased" (ver. 16).

I am within the veil with Christ,—outside the camp in the world, " bearing His reproach;" and, whilst thus delivered from the profession around me, that is not of Him, I am engaged in worship and doing good to all.

In regard to my hope, it is not, as people say, the " holding the doctrine of the second advent," but " waiting for God's Son from heaven." This is not a dead, dry doctrine. If we are really waiting for God's Son from heaven, we shall be sitting loose to the world.

I *have* Christ for my soul's need, and I am only " waiting for God's Son from heaven," for Christ to come from heaven to take His Church unto Himself, that where He is we may be also, and that may be this night. I am not looking for antichrist, for signs, for movements amongst the nations, but for this one holy, happy thing, I am waiting for God's Son from heaven. Oh do not let us be inconsistent, do not let us contradict that—seeking to grasp Christ with one hand, and hold fast the world with the other. If we know our position "within the veil," we must know our position "outside the camp," reproached, it may be, scorned, hated, suspected, of all who are not outside, but in the joy of fellowship with Him. "When Christ, who is our life, shall appear, we also then shall appear with Him in glory."

GOD IN EVERYTHING.

NOTHING so helps the Christian to endure the trials of his path, as the habit of seeing *God in everything*. There is no circumstance, be it ever so trivial or ever so common-place, which may not be regarded as a messenger from God, if only the ear be circumcised to hear, and the mind spiritual to understand the message. If we lose sight of this valuable truth, life, in many instances at least, will be but a dull monotony, presenting nothing beyond the most ordinary circumstances. On the other hand, if we could but remember, as we start each day on our course, that the hand of our Father can be traced in every scene—if we could see in the smallest, as well as in the most weighty circumstances, traces of the Divine presence, how full of deep interest would each day's history be found!

The book of Jonah illustrates this truth in a very marked way. There we learn, what we need so much to remember, that *there is nothing ordinary to the Christian;* every thing is extraordinary. The most commonplace things, the simplest circumstances, exhibit, in the history of Jonah, the evidences of special interference. To see this instructive feature, it is not needful to enter upon the detailed exposition of the book of Jonah, we only require to notice one expression, which occurs in it again and again: viz., "THE LORD PREPARED."

In chapter i. the Lord sends out a great wind into the sea, and this wind had in it a solemn voice for the prophet's ear, had he been wakeful to hear it. Jonah was the one who needed to be taught: for him the messenger was sent forth. The poor pagan mariners, no doubt, had often encountered a storm; to them it was nothing new, nothing special, nothing but what fell to the common lot of seamen; yet, it was special and extraordinary for one individual on board, though that one was asleep in the sides of the ship. In vain did the sailors seek to counteract the storm: nothing would avail until the Lord's message had reached the ears of him to whom it was sent.

Following Jonah a little farther, we perceive another instance of what we may term, GOD IN EVERYTHING. He is brought into new circumstances, yet he is not beyond the reach of the messengers of God. The Christian can never find himself in a position in which his Father's voice cannot reach his ear, or his Father's hand meet his view; for His voice can be heard, His hand seen in everything. Thus, when Jonah had been cast forth into the sea, "*the Lord prepared a great fish.*" Here, too, we see that there is nothing ordinary to the child of God. A great fish was nothing uncommon; there are many such in the sea; yet did the Lord *prepare* one for Jonah, in order that it might be the messenger of God to his soul.

Again, in chapter iv. we find the prophet sitting on the east side of the city of Nineveh, in sullenness and impatience, grieved because the city had not been overthrown, and entreating the Lord to take away his life. He would seem to have forgotten the lesson learnt during his three days' sojourn in the deep, and he therefore needed a fresh message from God: "And *the Lord prepared a gourd.*" This is very instructive. There was surely nothing uncommon in the mere circumstance of a gourd; other men might see a thousand gourds, and, moreover, might sit beneath their shade, and yet see nothing extraordinary in them. But Jonah's gourd exhibited traces of the hand of God, and forms a link, an important link, in the chain of circumstances through which, according to the design of God, the prophet was passing. The gourd now, like the great fish before, though very different in its kind, was the messenger of God to his soul. "So Jonah was exceeding glad of the gourd." He had before longed to depart, but his longing was more the result of impatience and chagrin, than of holy desire to depart and be at rest for ever. It was the painfulness of the present, rather than the happiness of the future, that made him wish to be gone.

This is often the case. We are frequently anxious to get away from present pressure; but if the pressure were removed, the longing would cease. If we longed for the coming of Jesus, and the glory of His blessed presence, circumstances would make no difference; we should then long as ardently to get away from circumstances of ease and sunshine, as from those of pressure and sorrow. Jonah, while he sat beneath the shadow of the gourd, thought not of departing, and the very fact of his being "exceeding glad of the gourd" proved how much he needed that special messenger from the Lord; it served to make manifest the true condition of his soul, when he uttered the words, "Take, I beseech thee, my life from me; for it is better for me to die than to live." The Lord can make even a gourd the instrument for developing the secrets of the human heart. Truly the Christian can say, *God is in everything.* The tempest roars, and the voice of God is heard; a gourd springs up in silence, and the hand of God is seen. Yet the gourd was but a link in the chain; for "*the Lord prepared a worm,*" and this worm, trifling as it was when viewed in the light of an instrument, was, nevertheless, as much the Divine agent as was the "great wind," or the "great fish." A worm, when used by God, can do wonders; it withered Jonah's gourd, and taught him, as it teaches us, a solemn lesson. True, it was only an insignificant agent, the efficacy of which depended upon its conjunction with others; but this only illustrates the more strikingly the greatness of our Father's mind. He can prepare a worm, and He can prepare a vehement east wind, and make them both, though so unlike, conducive to His great designs.

In a word, the spiritual mind sees *God in everything*. The worm, the whale, and the tempest, all are instruments in His hand. The most insignificant, as well as the most splendid agents, further His ends. The east wind would not have proved effectual, though it had been ever so vehement, had not the worm first done its appointed work. How striking is all this! Who would have thought that a worm and an east wind could be joint agents in doing a work of God? Yet so it was. Great and small are only terms in use amongst men, and cannot apply to Him "who humbleth Himself to behold the things that are in heaven," as well as "the things that are on earth." They are all alike to Him "who sitteth on the circle of the earth." Jehovah can tell the number of the stars, and while He does so He can take knowledge of a falling sparrow; He can make the whirlwind His chariot, and a broken heart His dwelling-place. Nothing is great or small with God.

The believer, therefore, must not look upon anything as ordinary, for God is in everything. True, he may have to pass through the same circumstances—to meet the same trials—to encounter the same reverses as other men; but he must not meet them in the same way, nor interpret them on the same principle; nor do they convey the same report to his ear. He should hear the voice of God, and heed His message in the most trifling as well as in the most momentous occurrence of the day. The disobedience of a child, or the loss of an estate, the obliquity of a servant, or the death of a friend, should all be regarded as Divine messengers to his soul.

So also, when we look around us in the world, God is in everything. The overturning of thrones, the crashing of empires, the famine, the pestilence, and every event that occurs amongst the nations, exhibit traces of the hand of God, and utters a voice for the ear of man. The devil will seek to rob the Christian of the real sweetness of this thought; he will tempt him to think that, at least, the commonplace circumstances of every-day life exhibit nothing extraordinary, but only such as happen to other men. But we must not yield to him in this. We must start on our course every morning, with this truth vividly impressed on our mind, *God is in everything*. The sun that rolls along the heavens in splendid brilliancy, and the worm that crawls along the path, have both alike been prepared of God, and, moreover, could both alike co-operate in the development of His unsearchable designs.

I would observe, in conclusion, that the only one who walked in the abiding remembrance of the above precious and important truth was our blessed Master. He saw the Father's hand, and heard the Father's voice, in everything. This appears pre-eminently in the season of the deepest sorrow. He came forth from the garden of Gethsemane with those memorable words, "The cup which my Father hath given me, shall I not drink it?" thus recognising in the fullest manner, that God is in everything.

THE SERPENT OF BRASS.

Read Numbers xxi. 4–9.

The magnificent song of Israel, in Exodus xv., had but too speedily been succeeded by the voice of murmuring and discontent. The roughness and privation of the wilderness soon obliterated from the minds of the children of Israel the remembrance of Jehovah's redeeming mercies. Past deliverance was forgotten under the sharpness of present pressure. "And they journeyed from mount Hor by the way of the Red Sea, to compass the land of Edom: and the soul of the people was much discouraged because of the way. And the people spake against God, and against Moses,

Wherefore have ye brought us up out of Egypt to die in the wilderness? for there is no bread, neither is there any water; and our soul loatheth this light bread." It was all well enough to escape out of Egypt, when the terrific judgments of God were falling upon it, in rapid succession. There was little attraction in the flesh-pots, the leeks, the onions, or the garlick, when they stood connected with the heavy plagues sent forth from the hand of an offended God. But now the plagues were forgotten, and the flesh-pots alone remembered. "Would to God we had died by the hand of the Lord in the land of Egypt, when we sat by the flesh-pots, and when we did eat bread to the full." What language! Man would rather sit by the flesh-pots, in a land of death and darkness, than walk with God through the wilderness, and eat bread from heaven! "Bread to the full," even though in Egypt, is better far, in man's estimation, than the unclouded presence of the God of glory. The Lord Himself had brought His glory down into connection with the very sand of the desert, because His redeemed were there. He had come down to bear with all their provocation—"to suffer their manners in the wilderness,"—all this grace and exceeding condescension might well have called forth in them a spirit of grateful and humble subjection. But no; the very earliest appearance of trial was sufficient to elicit from them the cry, "Would to God we had died in the land of Egypt!"

However, they were speedily made to taste the bitter fruits of their murmuring spirit. "And the Lord sent fiery serpents among the people, and they bit the people; and much people of Israel died." The serpent was the source of their discontent; and their condition, when bitten of the serpents, was fully calculated to reveal to them the true character of their discontent. If the Lord's people will not walk happily and contentedly with Him, they must taste the power of the serpent—alas! a terrible power, in whatever way it may be experienced.

The serpent's bite brought Israel to a sense of their sin. "Therefore the people came to Moses, and said, We have sinned, for we have spoken against the Lord, and against thee; pray unto the Lord, that He take away the serpents from us."

Here, then, was the moment for divine grace to act. Man's need has ever been the occasion for the display of God's grace and mercy. The moment Israel could say, "We have sinned," there was no further hindrance. God could act, and this was enough. When Israel murmured, the serpent's bite was the answer; when Israel confessed, God's grace was the answer. In the one case, the serpent was the instrument of their wretchedness; in the other, it was the instrument of their restoration and blessing. "And the Lord said unto Moses, make thee a fiery serpent, and set it upon a pole: and it shall come to pass that every one that is bitten, when he looketh upon it, shall live."

The very image of that which had done the mischief was set up, to be the channel through which divine grace might flow down in rich abundance to poor wounded sinners. Exquisite type of Christ upon the cross!

It is a very common error to view the Lord Jesus as the averter of the wrath of God only, rather than as the channel of His love. That He averts God's wrath, is, of course, most true; but He does far more; He has come down to open up the everlasting springs of the love of God to the heart of poor rebellious man. This makes a vast difference in the presentation of God's character to the sinner, which is of the utmost importance. Nothing can ever bring the sinner back to a state of holiness and happiness, but his being fully established in the consciousness of God's love. The very first effort of the serpent, when in the garden of Eden he assailed the creature, was to shake his confidence in God's kindness, and thus produce discontent with the place in which God had set him. Man's fall was the result of his doubting the love of God. Man's recovery must flow from his belief of that love; and it is the Son of God Himself that says, "God so loved the world, that He gave His only-begotten Son, that whosoever believeth in Him should not perish, but have everlasting life."

Now it is in close connection with this blessed statement that the Lord Jesus expressly teaches that He was the antitype of the brazen serpent.

As the Son of God sent forth from the Father, He was indeed the gift and expression of God's love to a perishing world. But He was also to be lifted up upon the cross in atonement for sin; and it was thus that Divine love met the necessities of the dying sinner. "As Moses lifted up the serpent in the wilderness, even so must the Son of man be lifted up; that whosoever believeth in Him should not perish, but have eternal life." The whole human family have felt the serpent's deadly sting; but the God of all grace has found a remedy, and, by the Holy Ghost sent down from heaven, calls on all who feel themselves bitten, to look to Jesus for life and peace. Christ is God's great ordinance, and through Him a full salvation is proclaimed to the sinner—a salvation so complete, so well based, so consistent with all the attributes of the Divine character, that Satan cannot raise a question about it. Resurrection is the Divine vindication of the work of the Cross, so that the believing soul may enjoy the most profound repose in reference to sin. God is well pleased in Jesus; and inasmuch as He views all believers in Him, He is well pleased in them also.

And, observe, faith is the instrument whereby the sinner lays hold of Christ's salvation. The wounded Israelite had simply to LOOK AND LIVE—look, not at himself—not at his wounds—not at others around him—not at anything else—but directly to God's remedy. If he refused to look to that, he had nought but death to expect.

Thus is it now. The sinner is called simply to look to Jesus. He is not told to look at his sins —to look at his righteousness—to look to ordinances—to look to churches—to look to men or angels—to none of these is he told to look, but exclusively to Jesus, whose death and resurrection form the eternal foundation of the believer's hope. God assures him, that "whosoever believeth in Him shall not perish, but have everlasting life." This should fully satisfy the heart and conscience. God is satisfied, and so ought we to be. To raise doubts is to deny the record of God. If an Israelite had said, "How do I know that looking to that serpent of brass will restore me?" or if he had begun to dwell upon the greatness and hopeless character of his malady, and to reason upon the apparent uselessness of looking up to God's ordinance; in short, if anything had prevented his looking to the brazen serpent, it would have involved a positive rejection of God, and death would have been the inevitable result. Thus, in the case of the sinner, the moment he is enabled to cast a look of faith at Jesus, his sins vanish. The blood of Jesus, like a mighty cleansing stream, flows over the conscience of the believer, and washes away every stain, and leaves him without spot, or wrinkle, or any such thing; and all this, too, in the very light of the holiness of God, where not a speck of sin can be tolerated.

THE BLIND MAN, AND THE PHARISEES WHO SAID "WE SEE."

Read John ix.

THE moral effect of the mission of Christ is strikingly presented in the 39th verse of this deeply interesting chapter. "And Jesus said, For judgment I am come into this world, that they which see not might see; and that they which see might be made blind." The work which He had just performed upon the blind man may be regarded as a very beautiful illustration of this statement, inasmuch as it was an illustration of the work of the Cross. The remedy which was applied to the blind man was one which the human judgment would at once pronounce to be the most likely to deprive a man of sight. "He spat on the ground, and made clay of the spittle, and He anointed the eyes of the blind man with the clay." This mode of acting was well calculated to confound human wisdom, and hence it leads one naturally to contemplate the great work of the Cross, in which we may behold the entire overthrow of all man's wisdom, and the full establishment of the wisdom of God upon its ruins. That a man crucified in weakness should be God's great ordinance of salvation to the believing soul—that this same man should, by death, destroy him that had the power of death—that He should, by being nailed to an accursed tree, become the foundation of eternal life to His Church,—all this involves a display of wisdom which, while it opens the eyes of poor blind sinners, and pours in the light of heavenly wisdom upon the dark understanding, only dazzles and confounds the learned and the wise of this world. "The foolishness of God is wiser than man."

But where are we to look for a manifestation of this "foolishness," which at once excels and confounds the wisdom of man? Assuredly to the Cross. "The preaching of the Cross is to the Greek foolishness." The proud sages of Greece, wrapped up in their schemes of philosophy, were but little prepared to understand or appreciate the preaching of the Cross, which called upon them to come down from their heights of fancied wisdom—to lay aside their philosophy as a vain and cumbrous mass of folly, and, as "poor and miserable and blind and naked" sinners, betake themselves to Him who had been nailed to the tree, between two malefactors.

Then, again, "the preaching of the Cross is to the Jew, a stumbling-block." The Jew would despise or stumble over the Cross, just as much as the Greek, though he looked at it from a totally different point of view. The Greek looked at the doctrine of the Cross from the fancied elevation of "science falsely so called." The Jew looked at it from amid the dark and bewildering mists of a traditionary religion. In both alike we behold the blinding power of the god of this age. Both alike were moving in a sphere which owned not "Christ crucified" as its centre.

Now, the Lord Jesus expressly tells the Pharisees in this chapter, that their sin was not their *real* blindness, but their *fancied* sight. "If ye were blind, ye should have no sin; but now *ye say*, We see; therefore your sin remaineth." A blind man could have his eyes opened; but for one who professed to see, no remedy was needed. A sick man may be made whole, but one who professes to be whole needs neither balm nor physician. The most hopeless feature in the condition of the Jews was their imagining that all was right. So far had they gone in their fancied soundness and rectitude, that they "had agreed already that if any man did confess that He (Jesus) was Christ, he should be put out of the synagogue." This was going very far. It was not that they had taken the trouble of investigating the claims of that blessed One who stood in their midst. No; without a question, they had made up their minds that no confessor of Christ should remain within the pale of *their* Church. How could they learn? What hope was there left for men, who, when called upon to look at an object and own its merits, would rise up, and in blind obstinacy close the window-shutters, or put a bandage across their eyes? None whatever. "Now ye say, We see; *therefore* your sin remaineth." This is truly solemn. The permanence of sin is connected with a mere profession to see. What a principle for an age of religious knowledge!

But let us trace in the person of the blind man the progress of an honest soul upon whom the light of heaven had dawned.

From the moment that this man became the subject of the work of Christ, he was a marked man. "The neighbours therefore, and they which before had seen him that he was blind, said, Is not this he that sat and begged?" The marked change that had taken place was manifest to all who had known aught of his previous state. It was an important case, and one which needed to be submitted to the judgment of the Church. "They brought to the Pharisees him that aforetime was blind." Nothing could be accredited which wanted the stamp of the Church's approval. It was in vain that a blind man had had his eyes opened to see the light of heaven. If the matter met not the approval of the Pharisees, it must go for nought. Now let us see how the Pharisees deal with the case. They were, we feel assured, ready to bear with anything save a clear, simple, emphatic testimony to the work of Christ; but this was the very thing which the man was about to lay before them. "How were thine eyes opened?" Mark the reply, "*He* put clay on mine eyes." How little the Pharisees knew, or cared to know, of this! They, no doubt, regarded the matter as an insult to common sense. It certainly was, in its way, "a stone of stumbling" to them.

But who did the man mean by "He"? Who was "He"? This was the point. The poor man was ignorant of this himself, though he was on the highway to intelligence about it. He knew the *work*, but not the *Person* of Christ. Yet how highly distinguished was he, in being led to a knowledge of the work of Christ; yea, in being himself the subject of it; for this is the true way in which to arrive at a knowledge of it. Intellectual accuracy in reference to the plan of salvation is but a poor, cold, uninfluential thing, when not accompanied with the personal experience of its efficacy. We shall certainly never be able thereby to confound the logic of such as stand up merely for the defence of systematic religion, apart from, or in opposition to, Christ. We must be able to show, in our own persons, our character, our ways, the practical results of the work of Christ, or else all our accuracy will be little worth. "He put clay on mine eyes, and I washed, *and do see.*" Here was the presentation of a living fact which was calculated to bear down with greater weight upon a Pharisee's conscience, than all the arguments that could be used. What could gainsay it? Men might reason as they pleased; they might even talk about giving glory to God; but this man could prove in his own person, that the work of Christ had done that for him which the Jewish system, with its priesthood and its rites, never could. This was enough for him, and it would have been enough, too, for any who were not blinded by the power of system.

But, observe, how the heart of this poor man

lingers about the work of Jesus. He never allows himself to be drawn away from it, in order to follow the puzzling arguments of the Pharisees. To all their questionings and reasonings his reply is, "He put clay on mine eyes, and I washed and do see." Here was his solid ground, from which no logic could shake him. He kept to the simple fact of Christ's work, and reasoned not upon it, and this was his security. Had he reasoned upon it, they would have confounded him, for they were subtle men; but they could make nothing of his simple testimony to the fact of what Christ had done for him. "One thing I know, that whereas I was blind, now I see." The connection between the two statements is very marked. "He put clay on mine eyes," and "now I see." When we can connect the work of Christ with positive results in our own case, the testimony is irresistible; but there is a feebleness and a shallowness in the testimony of such as merely apprehend intellectually the theory of the gospel, which, not being connected with any positive result in the character and conduct, is soon borne down by the enemies of truth. This is very perceptible in the case of the parents of the man. They, when questioned, could deliver but a poor cold testimony in the matter. So far as their son and his wretchedness were concerned, they could speak distinctly enough, "but by what means he now seeth, we know not; or who hath opened his eyes, we know not." In other words, they neither knew nor cared to know Christ or His work. They valued their position in connection with the accredited religion of the day, and were not prepared to bear the reproach of throwing in their lot with Christ and His followers. This, alas! is but too common. It requires no ordinary depth of truth in the soul, to enable a man to "go without the camp" to Jesus. It must be a personal question. The grace of God as manifested in the cross must be experimentally known, else we never shall be able to witness a good confession. The name of Jesus never was, nor is it now, popular in the world. Religiousness may be, and doubtless will. But religiousness is one thing, and the faithful confession of Christ is quite another. The Pharisees and chief priests had plenty of religion; yea, they were its guardians. They could say, "This man is not of God, because he keepeth not the Sabbath-day;" and again, "Give God the praise; we know that this man is a sinner." All this sounded very religiously; but, my reader, we must ever bear in mind, that, to talk of giving glory to God, or of honouring His institutions, while Jesus is rejected, is the merest delusion. Jesus is God's great institution, and the cross of Jesus is that which makes His person and work available to the sinner; hence, if he be rejected, we are destitute of the only true and divinely recognised basis of religion. One divine thought about God's anointed Saviour is better far than all the devout expressions of fleshy pietism. Where Jesus is known, there is the preparedness of heart to suffer for His name, and also the true desire to be identified with Him, and conformed to Him. But the parents of the man had not this preparedness of heart, and hence their testimony was characterized by all that so-called prudent caution which is ever observable in mere worldly religionists. "These words spake his parents, because they feared the Jews; for the Jews had agreed already, that if any man did confess that he was Christ, he should be put out of the synagogue." This was a serious affair. The Jewish system had, of course, a large place in the affections of every pious Jew, nor would any one lightly give up his position as a member of it; still less would he think of attaching himself to the person of one who was manifestly outside of all that which the world deemed reputable or desirable.

However, the man whose eyes were opened, "Could not but speak the thing he had seen and heard," and the consequence was, that the religious guides of the people could not endure the edge of his simple testimony—a testimony based throughout upon the work of Christ. He had received light, and this light had come into collision with the darkness. There could be no harmony—no fellowship—no rest. The light must be put out. So long as he had been a blind member of their system, it was well. They never raised a question; but since he had received light, and was not disposed to put it under a bushel, nor yet to put his conscience into their keeping, they had only to seek to get rid of him, as best they could. "Thou wast altogether born in sins, and dost thou teach us? And they cast him out." They were the great depositaries of knowledge, and he was but a poor ignorant man, and should not presume to think for himself, or set up his judgment in opposition to them. They, no doubt, regarded him as an obstinate heretic, for whom nothing was reserved saved the thunders of the Church. "They cast him out." And why? Simply because he had had his eyes opened. How strange! But yet how like what we see around us! How often do we see, now, cases like this! Men go on living in vice and ignorance, yet tolerated by human religion; but the moment the holy light of Scripture dawns upon them, they are only deemed fit subjects for the rack and the stake. The vilest crimes are light, in the judgment of a corrupt religious system, when compared with the honest confession of the name of Christ.

We have already noticed the extent of this honest man's intelligence. It only extended to the work of Christ. He understood nothing of his Person as yet. This knowledge was reserved for him when cast forth without the pale of the synagogue. "Jesus heard that they had cast him out; and when he had found him, he said unto him, Dost thou believe on the Son of God? He answered, *Who is He*, Lord, that I might believe on Him?" Now there is something very instructive in this progress in intelligence. He had been cast, by reason of his faithfulness, into a position of decided sympathy with the Son of God. The Good Shepherd had, in tender mercy, visited the fold, and was now calling this His sheep by name, that He might lead him forth into a wide and wealthy place, wherein he might taste the blessedness of fellowship with that "one flock" which was about to be placed in the Father's hand for ever. "Who is He?" Precious inquiry of an honest heart! An inquiry speedily answered indeed. "Thou hast both seen Him, and it is He that talketh with thee. And he said, Lord, I believe, and he worshipped Him." Here, then, we may well leave this highly favoured soul—favoured, though expelled from amid all that was highly esteemed amongst men. Truly happy was it for him to find himself outside a system which was rapidly crumbling to ruin, and to know his place as a worshipper at the feet of the Son of God. He had gone without the camp to Jesus, bearing His reproach, and is now seen offering the sacrifice of praise, even the fruit of his lips.

My reader, may we know and prove, in our own persons, the practical application of all this!

LAW AND GRACE EXEMPLIFIED.

Read Deut. xxi. 18—21, and Luke xv. 11—32.

IN looking through the various laws and ordinances of the Old Testament, we cannot fail to observe the intense spirit of holiness which they breathe; the most trifling ordinance, apparently, was calculated to impress Israel with a sense of holiness. God's presence in their midst was ever to be the spring of holiness and separation to His people. Hence we read, in this passage of the book of Deuteronomy, "So shalt thou put away evil from among you." And again, in the ordinance of the manslayer, we read, "Defile not, therefore, the land which ye shall inhabit, wherein I dwell: for I the Lord dwell among the children of Israel." (Numb. xxxv. 34.) *God's dwelling place must be holy;* and "without holiness no man shall see the Lord." There can be no alteration in this. Dispensations may change, but God, blessed be His name, can never cease to be "the holy, holy, holy Lord God of Israel;" nor can He ever cease in His effort to make His people like what He is Himself. Whether He speak from amid the thunders of mount Sinai, or in all the gentleness and grace of the blood-sprinkled mercy-seat in the heavens, His object is still the same,—viz., to make and keep His people holy.

Very different, however, is the mode of acting

in the law, from that which we find in the gospel. In the law, God was calling upon man to be what He desired him to be; He set before him a high and holy standard, no doubt, but yet a standard to which man could not attain. Even though he might aspire most ardently after what the law set before him, yet, from the very fact of what he was, he could not attain to it. All his efforts were based upon the unholiness of a nature which was perfectly irrecoverable. The law was like a mirror, let down from heaven, to show to all who would only look honestly into it, that they were, both negatively and positively, the very thing which the law condemned and set aside. The law said, "Do this," and "Thou shalt not do that," and man's only response, uttered from the very depth of his nature, was, "Oh wretched man that I am!" In short, the law, like a plumb-line, measured the human character, and showed out all its crookedness and imperfection. It was not, by any means, its province to make the sinner better. No; its province was to reveal his sins, and put him under the curse. "The law entered, that the offence might abound." And again, "As many as are of the works of the law are under the curse." This is very plain. Have anything to do with the law, and it will prove you to be a poor helpless sinner, and put you under the curse. It can really do nothing else, so long as God and man, holiness and sin, continue to be what they are. We may seek to confound law and grace, in our ignorance of the true genius of each; but it will prove, in the end, to be most thoroughly vain. As well might we seek to cause light and darkness to mingle, as to make law and grace combine. No; they are as distinct as any two things can be. The law can only point out to man the error of his ways—the evil of his nature. It does not make him straight, but only tells him he is crooked; it does not make him clean, but only tells him he is defiled. Nor was the law designed, as is often imagined, to lead sinners to Christ. This idea is founded upon an erroneous quotation of Galatians iii. 24. It is not said, "The law was our schoolmaster to bring us unto Christ," but "the law was our schoolmaster unto (or until) Christ." The words, "to bring us" are in italics, and do not appear in the original. This is important, as helping my reader to understand the nature, object, and scope of the law. How could the law bring a man to Christ? All it did for him was to shut him up under the curse; his finding his way to Christ was the result of quite another ministry altogether. The law acted the part of a schoolmaster from the time it was given until Christ came, by keeping souls under a restraint from which nothing could deliver, save the spirit of liberty imparted through the gospel of Christ.

However, by a simple comparison of the two Scriptures which stand at the head of this paper, we shall have a very striking proof of the difference between the law and the Gospel. The case presented in each, is that of a son who was disposed to do his own will and enjoy his own way. This is no uncommon case. The prodigal desired to have his portion, and to be away from under the eye of his father. But, ah! how soon he was called to learn his folly! "When he had spent all, there arose a mighty famine in that land, and he began to be in want." Just so; how else could it be? He had left the only place in which all his need could be supplied, even the father's house. He had made his portion and the father's to be separate things; and hence he was compelled to learn that the former was capable of being exhausted. We can get to the bottom of all human circumstances and resources. There never was a cup of human or earthly happiness—be it ever so deep—ever so abundant in desirable ingredients—which could not be drained to the bottom. There never was a well of human, or earthly refreshment, of which it could not be said, "He that drinketh of this water shall thirst again." Not so, however, with the cup which redeeming love puts into our hand—not so with the wells of salvation from which the Gospel invites us to draw. These are exhaustless, eternal, divine. As the countless ages of eternity roll along, God's cup shall be full, and his wells shall send forth their streams in immortal freshness and purity. My reader, how sweet—how ineffably sweet—to partake of these!

But the prodigal "began to be in want." And

what then? Did he think of the father? No. So long as he had any other resource, he would not think of returning home. "He went and joined himself to a citizen of that country, and he sent him into his fields to feed swine." This was terrible. Thus does Satan crush the spirits of his votaries. Every one who is not walking in communion with God and subjection to the Gospel of Christ, is thus engaged in the service of Satan. There is no middle ground. Reader, who are you serving? Are you serving Christ or Satan? If the latter, oh *remember the end.* Remember, too, the Father's love—the Father's house. Remember that "God willeth not the death of a sinner, but rather that he should turn from his evil ways and live." This you may learn from the prodigal. The moment his necessities led him to think of returning home, that home was open wide to receive him. And observe, it was simply *his need* that caused him to say, "I will arise and go to my father." It was not any longing desire for the father's company, but merely for the father's bread. Many are vainly looking within for some rising emotions of affectionate desire after God, not knowing that our very necessities—our very miseries—our very sins render us suited objects for the exercise of Divine grace. *Grace* suits *the miserable*, because the miserable can magnify grace.

And here we have arrived at a point, at which we may appreciate the contrast between our Scriptures. How would the law have dealt with our prodigal? The answer is simple. "Then shall his father and his mother lay hold on him, bring him out unto the elders of his city, and unto the gate of his place. And they shall say unto the elders of his city, This our son is stubborn and rebellious, he will not obey our voice; he is a glutton and a drunkard. And all the men of the city shall stone him with stones, that he die; so shalt thou put away evil from among you; and all Israel shall hear and fear." The law could speak of nought but judgment and death. Mercy was not within its range, nor at all in accordance with its spirit. "The soul that sinneth it shall die," was its stern language. And again, "Cursed is every one that continueth not in all things which are written in the book of the law to do them."

But how does grace deal with its object? Oh, for hearts to adore our God, who is the fountain of grace! "But when he was yet a great way off, his father saw him, and had compassion, and ran and fell on his neck and kissed him." In short, the mode of treatment is the very opposite. The law said, "Lay hold on him"—the Gospel said, "Embrace him;" the law said, "Stone him"—the Gospel said, "Kiss him;" and yet, be it remembered, we meet the same God in both. The God of Israel speaks both in Deuteronomy and in Luke; and, moreover, we must remember what has already been stated, viz., that we trace the same object in both, which is, to give full deliverance from the power of evil. The stone of judgment and the embrace of love were both designed to put away evil; but ah! how much more fully was the latter in sympathy with the Divine mind, than the former! Judgment is truly God's strange work. It was far more congenial to Him to be on the neck of the poor returning prodigal, than to be within the enclosure of mount Sinai. True, the prodigal had nothing to commend him—he had proved himself to be all that the law condemned,—he had been "a glutton and a drunkard"—the rags of the far country were upon him, and, were the law but to take its course, instead of the affectionate embrace of love, he would have to meet the stern grasp of justice; and instead ot the father's kiss, he would have had to meet the stone of judgment from the men of his city, in the presence of the elders. Hence we see the contrast between law and grace—it is most striking.

But here, let us ask, how could all this be? How can we reconcile the marvellous difference in the principles of acting here set before us? Whither must we turn for a solution of this apparent contradiction? How can God embrace a poor sinner? How can He shield such from the full action of justice and the law? In other words, how can He be "just and the justifier"? How can He pardon the sinner steeped to the lips in iniquity, and yet not "clear the guilty"? How can He, who "cannot look upon sin," but with abhorrence, and "in whose sight the heavens are not clean," sit down at the table with a poor wretched prodigal? Where, my reader, shall we find an answer to these questions? *In the cross of Calvary.* Yes: there we have a precious—a divine reply to all. The Man nailed to the tree settles everything. Jesus bore sin's tremendous curse upon the cross—He exposed His own bosom to the stroke of justice—He drained to the dregs the cup of Jehovah's righteous wrath—"He bore our sins in His own body on the tree"—"He hath made Him to be sin for us, who knew no sin, that we might be made the righteousness of God in Him." Was not this a vindication of the law? Did ever the words, "So shalt thou put evil away," fall with such impressive solemnity upon the ear, as when the blessed Son of God cried out, from amid the horrors of Golgotha, "My God, my God, why hast thou forsaken me?" Oh! never, never. All the stones that were ever cast at offending sinners—all the penalties that were ever inflicted—yea, we shall proceed further and say, that the eternal punishment of the wicked in the lake of fire, could not afford such a solemn proof of God's hatred of sin, as the scene on the cross. There it was that men and angels might behold God's thoughts of sin, and God's thoughts of sinners. His hatred of the former, and His love for the latter. The very same act which shows out the condemnation of sin, shows out the salvation of the sinner. Hence the Cross, while it most fully vindicates the holiness and justice of God, opens up a channel through which the copious streams of redeeming love can flow down to the guilty sinner. "Mercy and truth met together; righteousness and peace kissed each other," when the Son of God offered up Himself as a sacrifice for sin.

And, if it be asked, What proof have we of this? What solid ground of assurance have we of the full forgiveness and perfect acceptance of the believer? The answer is, *Resurrection.* Jesus is now at the right hand of the majesty in the heavens; and there, moreover, on behalf of the believer. "He was delivered for our offences," and could we go no further than this, we might despair; but, it is added, "He was raised again for our justification." Here we have full peace—full emancipation—full victory. When God raised Jesus from the dead, He declared Himself as "the God of peace." Justice was satisfied, and the sinner's surety was set down at God's right hand; and all who, by the operation of the Holy Ghost, believe in His death and resurrection, are looked at in Him, and seen to be as free from every charge of sin as He is. Most marvellous grace! Who could have conceived such a thing? Who could have thought that He, who is "the brightness of God's glory, and the express image of His person," should come down and put Himself in the sinner's place, and bear all the wrath, curse, and judgment due to sin, in order that the sinner might be set down in the very presence of the holiness of God, without "spot or wrinkle or any such thing," so that God might be able to say of him, "Thou art all fair, there is no spot in thee"? My reader, was ever love like this? Truly we have here, love in its fountain—love in its channel—and love in its application. The Father is the eternal fountain, the Son is the channel, and the Holy Ghost is the power of application. What divine completeness! What perfect peace! What a solid resting-place for the sinner! Who can raise a question? God has received His prodigal—has clothed and adorned him—killed the fatted calf for him—and above all, has given utterance to the words, "*It is meet* that *we* should make merry and be glad"—words which ought to dispel every shadow of fear and doubt from the heart. If God can say, in virtue of the finished work of Christ, "It is meet," who can say it is not meet? Satan may accuse, but God's reply is, "Is not this a brand plucked out of the fire?" In short, the soul that believes in Jesus is lifted into a perfectly cloudless region, where, it may be truly said, "there is neither enemy, nor evil occurrent;" and in that region we can see no one so exquisitely happy in the divine results of redemption, as the blessed God Himself. If the prodigal could possibly have retained a feeling of doubt or reserve, what could have so effectually banished it as the father's joy in getting him back again? Neither doubt nor fear can live in the light of our Father's reconciled countenance. If we believe that God rejoices in receiving back a sinner, we cannot harbour suspicion or hesitancy. It is not merely that God *can* receive us, but it is His joy to do so. Hence we not only know that "grace *reigns* through righteousness," but that all heaven rejoices in one repenting sinner. Thanks be unto God for His unspeakable gift.

And now, one word, in conclusion, as to the way in which God secures holiness through grace. Is sin made light of? Is it tolerated? Does the blessed God, when He receives a returning prodigal to His bosom, in sovereign grace, without one upbraiding look or expression, lead us to suppose that sin has become a whit less odious or abominable? By no means. We have already seen how the Cross has added force and solemnity to every one of the divine statutes against sin. God has proved, by the bruising of His beloved Son, that His hatred of sin was only to be equalled by His love for the sinner. *A crucified Christ*, declares God's hatred of sin; *a risen Christ* declares the triumph of His love for the sinner. The death of Christ vindicates the law; His resurrection emancipates the soul of the believer, while both these together, form the basis of all practical holiness, as we learn in the 6th chapter of Romans. "How shall we that are dead to sin, live any longer therein?" "We are buried with Him by baptism into death; that, like as Christ was raised from the dead by the glory of the Father, so we also should walk in newness of life." "That the body of sin might be destroyed, that we should no longer serve sin." When the father received the prodigal, he did so in a way altogether worthy of himself, and of the honour of his house. He could not receive him otherwise. He could not allow him to continue in the rags of the far country, nor in the habits thereof either. The husks and the rioting had all to be laid aside. His dress and habits were now to correspond with his new position. *Fellowship with the father* henceforth became his grand characteristic. He was not put under a dry code of rules as a servant, as he himself had sought to be. No; the manner of his reception, the principle on which he was to be dealt with, and the position to be assigned him were all in the father's power, and, being in his power, we can easily see what his *will* was. He should either be received with a kiss or not at all; he should either be seated at the table or not enter the house at all; he should either get the place of a son or nothing. In short, it was the father's grace that arranged all for the prodigal, and happy was it for him to have it so.

But, oh! how could the prodigal think lightly of sin in the light of such extraordinary grace? Impossible. He was most effectually delivered from the power of sin by the grace which reigned in his reception, and in his position. It was truly such as to set sin before him in the most fearful colours. "Shall we sin because we are not under the law, but under grace? God forbid." Yes, God forbid. It cannot, it must not be, my reader. Grace has set us free, free not only from the penalty of sin, but free from its power—free from its present dominion. Blessed freedom! The law gave sin power over the sinner; grace gives him power over it. The law revealed to the sinner his weakness, grace makes him acquainted with the strength of Christ; the law put the sinner under the curse, no matter who or what he was; grace, introduces him into all the ineffable blessedness of the Father's house—the Father's bosom; the law elicited only the cry, "O wretched man that I am;" grace enables him to sing triumphantly, "Thanks be to God who giveth us the victory." These are important differences, and such as may well lead us into deep thankfulness for the truth that "we are not under the law, but under grace."

If anything was needed to prove that nothing but grace can form the basis of holy service, the spirit and bearing of the elder brother in our beautiful parable would most fully prove it. He thought he had ever been a very faithful servant, and his heart rebelled against the high position assigned to his younger brother. But alas! he understood not the father's heart. It was not the cold service of formalism or legalism that was needed, but the service of love—the service of one who felt he had been forgiven much—or rather those deep affections which flow from the sense of redeeming love. All practical Christianity is comprehended in that word of the apostle, viz., "We love Him because He first loved us." God grant that we may all enter more into the sacred power of these simple, but most precious truths.

THE LORD OUR SHEPHERD.

(Luke xv. 1–7.)

It is ever soothing to the spirit to ponder the character of the Lord Jesus as our Shepherd, in whatever aspect of that character we view Him; whether as "the *good* Shepherd," laying down His life for the sheep; or "the *great* Shepherd," coming up out of the grave, having, in the greatness of His strength, deprived death of its deadly sting, and the grave of its victory; or lastly, as "the *chief* Shepherd," when, surrounded by all His subordinate shepherds, who from love to His adorable person, and, through the grace of His Spirit, have watched over and cared for the flock, He shall wreathe the brow of each with a diadem of glory. In any or all of these stages of our Divine Shepherd's history, it is happy and edifying to consider Him. Indeed, there is something in our Lord's character as Shepherd, which is peculiarly adapted to our present condition. Through grace we have been constituted "the people of His pasture and the sheep of His hand;" and, as such, it is a shepherd we specially need. As *sinners*, ruined and guilty, we need Him as the "Lamb of God;" His atoning blood meets us at that point in our history, and satisfies our utmost need. As *worshippers*, we need Him as our "great High-Priest," whose robes, the varied expression of His attributes and qualifications, most blessedly prove to our souls how effectually He fills that office. As *disciples*, we need Him in His character as teacher, "in whom are hid *all* the treasures of wisdom and knowledge." But, as *sheep*, exposed to countless dangers in our passage through this dark wilderness, in this "gloomy and dark day," we truly stand in need of the friendly voice of our Shepherd, whose rod and staff give security and stability to our footsteps as we journey onward to the heavenly fold.

Now, in these verses that I have read for you, we find the shepherd presented to us in a deeply interesting stage of his gracious work; he is here seen *in search of the sheep*. The parable derives peculiar force from the fact that it was put forth, together with the parables of the *lost* piece of silver, and the *lost* son, as an argument in favour of God's gracious actings towards sinners. God, in the person of the Lord Jesus, had come so very near to *the sinner*, that legalism and Pharisaism, as represented by the scribes and Pharisees, took offence at it. "This man *receiveth sinners*, and eateth with them." Here was the offence of which Divine grace stood charged at the bar of man's legal, proud, self-righteous heart. But it was the very glory of God—God manifest in the flesh—God come down to earth thus to receive sinners. It was for that

He came down into a ruined world. He left not the throne and bosom of His Father to come down here to search for righteous people; for wherefore should He search for them? Who would think of going to look for anything but that which was "*lost*"? Surely the very presence of Christ in the world proved that He had come *in search of something*, and, moreover, that that something must have been "*lost*." "The Son of man came to *seek* and to *save* that which was *lost*." The soul should greatly rejoice in the fact that it was as a *lost* thing that it drew forth the grace and pity of the shepherd's heart. We may inquire what it was that could have drawn the heart of Jesus towards such as we are; yes, we may inquire, but eternity alone will unfold to us the answer to the inquiry. We might ask the shepherd in this parable why he thought more about the one solitary *lost* sheep than he did about the ninety and nine which were not lost at all. What would have been his answer? "The *lost* one is my object, it is valuable to *me*, and I *must* find it." So it was with the merchantman, who surely is no other than Jesus: he alone could see, in that which lay buried in the bowels of the earth, an object which was worth everything to him: Jesus alone could see, in a helpless sinner, an object for which He thought it worth stooping from His Father's bright throne to save:—

"He saw me ruined in the fall,
Yet loved me, notwithstanding all;
He saved me from my lost estate;
His loving-kindness, oh, how great!"

We may well wonder at the mystery of Christ's love to the Church; it will be a subject of wonder to angels and saints for ever. But while we can never solve the profound mystery, nor fathom the depths of redeeming love, how sweet to the poor sin-harassed soul to know itself as the object of such love! Yes; it is at once soothing and elevating; moreover, it is the only true basis of real holiness and devotedness of heart to God. "We love Him *because* He *first* loved us." God must have the first place in redemption, seeing the whole plan had its origin in His eternal mind; it emanated from Him. The poor, silly, straying sheep could never devise a way for its return to the fold from which it had gone forth. How could it, when the very same disposition which had led it at first to wander would make it a wanderer to the end? How could the disposition which at first led the creature to revolt from under the hand of his God ever engender a spirit of subjection, or a spirit of confidence afterwards? Impossible. Hence the force of the words, "*Go after* that which is *lost.*"

In these few words we have the grand action of redemption, and the attitude of God therein. God, in redemption, is emphatically and pre-eminently *the seeker*, and not the *sought*. This we are taught in Genesis iii. The words, "Where art thou?" fully show us God "*going after* that which was *lost.*" Man had fled away from the face of God; he had indeed "gone astray,"—he had sought to find a hiding-place, not *in*, but *from* God, behind the trees of the garden: and when the blessed God came down to visit man, He found Himself quite alone, as far as man was concerned; and, moreover, He had, thus *alone*, to begin again, not merely to *create* but to *redeem*. In creation, it was Omnipotence acting upon unresisting matter; but in redemption, it was boundless love and grace dealing with a rebel heart and a ruined creation. Hence the grand inference involving a truth at once most simple and sublime, namely, GOD IS SEEN AS MUCH MOVING ALONE IN REDEMPTION AS HE IS IN CREATION. Man was not in the scene when God called worlds into existence; he was not there when the finger of Omnipotence set yonder sun in the heavens to run its great annual course; he was not there when a bound was set to the angry billows, that they might not pass the Divine decree. No; man was not there, nor could be: he was then in the dust of the earth, and could take no part in the grand transactions that were being developed; and yet, such is the wild infatuation of the human heart, that, although redemption must be admitted to be a more difficult (if it be allowable to speak of anything as difficult in reference to God), a more godlike work than creation, yet he will vainly and presumptuously intrude into that scene where God is, in solitary dignity, carrying out the first plan of redemption —a plan in which He alone could act. "No man can by any means redeem his brother, nor give to

God a ransom for him, for the redemption of his soul is precious, and it ceaseth for ever." Redemption is too precious a work for God to give into the hands of any one; He himself must have *all* the joy, all the glory of saving poor self-destroyed sinners. Just so is it in these verses which we are looking at. The shepherd is *alone* in the pursuit.

The sheep knew nothing about the loving anxiety of the shepherd's heart; nothing of the motives that had led him forth in this self-denying search. No, these things were unknown to the sheep. The shepherd did not seek the co-operation of the sheep in his search, such would have been useless. The sheep was wandering away from the fold, and would have wandered on till overtaken by the wolf, had not the tender heart of the shepherd led him to seek it amid the wild labyrinths of the desert. And oh, what unwearied grace breathes in the words "*until he find it*"! Jesus, our gracious Shepherd, would not allow Himself to be baffled in the work which He had undertaken. He came fully prepared to meet all the obstacles that stood in His way; He was fully aware of all that lay before Him ere He could lay His hand upon the *lost* one. He knew that He had to encounter all the malignant opposition of Satan, who would dispute every step of the way with Him. He knew what enmity existed in the heart of the very creature He had come to seek and to save; and, above all, He had fully before His mind the cup of ineffable bitterness, which was prepared for Him at the cross, even the hiding of God's countenance; the three darkest hours that had ever passed over the soul of an intelligent being, more terrible to His divinely sensitive soul than all the sorrow and trial He had encountered at the hand of man or Satan.

Did He, then, shrink from encountering Satan? Nay, He, as "the stronger man," penetrated into the very heart of the strong man's palace, and spoiled him of "all his armour wherein he trusted."—"By death, He destroyed him that had the power of death." Did He grow weary of man's ceaseless and deadly enmity, or was He driven back by it? No; He moved onward in all the Divine fortitude of love, bursting through maze after maze of human opposition, until at last, when man had poured forth all the deadly Satanic poison that was in his heart, and had nailed the heavenly Shepherd to the cursed tree, He graciously breathed the prayer, "Father, forgive them," and poured forth the *blood*, by virtue of which the prayer could be and was answered.

Further, did death drive Him back from His purpose of mercy? No, "He met its deadly sting;" it was to Him indeed a terrible sting, yet He bore it, and, by bearing it, robbed it of all its power to sting the soul that believes on Him. Did the grave—"the horrible pit and the miry clay"—deter His soul? No; He went down into the very heart of the grave, into the innermost parts of the kingdom of death, and there shook it to its very centre; and, as if the realms of death had already felt the rumblings of the tremendous earthquake by which they were about to be shaken, the grave opened its mouth to set free from its grasp its long-held prey, just as the Prince of life was about to descend into it. In a word, nothing could stop the Divine Shepherd in His search for "that which was lost, *until He found it.*" This is truly Divine. God, in creation, could not be hindered in the accomplishment of His great designs, but compelled matter to yield to the power of His voice; and then, when Satan had marred creation, and God was called upon in the vindication of His name to ascend the loftier heights of redemption, we may follow Him in His wondrous upward path from height to height, until we hear those soul-stirring words, "*I have found* my sheep which was *lost.*" Blessed announcement! "*I have found.*" It is the full triumph of redeeming love over all the power of Satan.

And mark, here, two important features of our shepherd's love, namely, *uncomplaining* and *unupbraiding.* We hear not a syllable about all his trouble in searching for the sheep, the time, the distance, or the labour involved. Not a word. On the contrary, the impression left on the mind by those verses is, that the shepherd considered himself amply repaid for all his trouble when he had the stray one once more within his grasp.

So it is with our "Good Shepherd," "who for the joy that was set before Him, endured the cross, despising the shame." What joy? The joy of being able to say "I have found." There was no such joy in creation; all that God could say in creation was, "I have made;" it was reserved for the more glorious and sublime scheme of redemption to admit the higher note, "*I have found.*" The former was said, as it were, at *this* side of the grave; the latter, at the *other* side. Creation left man within the reach of Satan's arrows, which can wound in all places on this side of the grave; redemption brings us beyond the grave, and, as a consequence, beyond the reach of Satan's arrows. Again, the love expressed in these verses, is an un-upbraiding love. The shepherd does not reproach the sheep, nor begin in anger to *drive* it home. Ah, no! the heart—the tender, compassionate, sympathizing heart of Jesus is seen here—the heart of Him who, standing amid the mighty wreck of human things, and contemplating the sad and wide-spread desolation which Satan had caused in God's creation, could shed a tear of deep pity for the misery which He alone, by and in resurrection, could alleviate.

And where, I would ask, do we find the loveliest exhibition of this un-upbraiding love? At the first meeting between the Lord and His apostles after the resurrection; yes, there we see it indeed; instead of reproaching them for what they no doubt felt to have been a base desertion of their dear Lord, in the hour of His deepest anguish, His words are, "Peace be unto you." Oh! what a thorough confounding of Satan is here, what a calm conviction that Satan was the grand cause of all the mischief, breathes through those words; incomparable grace! May it bind our souls, beloved friends, to Him who is the great fountain and channel thereof.

But what does the shepherd do with the sheep? Does he rest satisfied with merely having found it? No; there was something far beyond this: to find it was but the first step as regards the application of the shepherd's love and care to the sheep; it was but the beginning of the wondrous journey of this once lost but now found sheep. The sheep, as we read, was away in the wilderness, the shepherd found it, and it would be an important question as to how it was to be conducted home; nor does the shepherd leave this question long unsettled, for he no sooner finds the sheep than he puts it in the most secure place, "*he layeth it on his shoulders.*" How? complaining of the weight, or the trouble? Oh no: "he layeth it on his shoulders *rejoicing.*" How little the sheep knew of the deep emotions of joy which were filling the soul of the shepherd; it would probably augment his trouble by kicking, plunging, and struggling to tumble off its place of security and rest: but no matter for that, the shepherd had hold of it, and therein he rejoiced. A loving heart and a powerful shoulder could surmount all obstacles. And how simple and sweet is the application of this to our adorable Shepherd! "Having loved His own which were in the world, He loved them unto the end," is the testimony of the Spirit about Him. The love of Christ was not a love that could be exhausted, or in the least degree cooled or lessened by personal experience of the unloveliness of the object; He knew what He could and would make of His church, even "a glorious Church, not having spot or wrinkle or any such thing," and, He stopped not short of the grand consummation of the Church's beauty and glory "in the dispensation of the fulness of times." This is the true principle of love. If we were in the habit of dwelling on what Christians *will* be, and not what they *are*, *i.e.* in themselves, our love would be of a purer and more permanent character.

But what security we have expressed in the words, "He layeth it on his shoulders!" This is the place of the weakest believer in Jesus. He is on the shoulders of Him who had power to burst asunder the gates of brass—Him who had vanquished Satan, death, and hell, and who, consequently, cannot meet with any opposing power equal to His own. Hence His own comforting words, "No man is able to pluck them out of my hand." Surely we may say, in the triumphant language of the apostle, "Who shall separate us?"

Finally, observe the words, "*When he cometh home.*" Here we have the highest point in this truly interesting and evangelical narrative. There could be no calling together of the friends and neighbours *in the wilderness*. No, the wilderness is the place for drawing forth Divine love in seeking, and Divine power in saving the lost; the wilderness must be the scene of the shepherd's anxiety and toil, because it is a place of danger to the sheep. There is something particularly beautiful in this little narrative; so natural, yet so Divine. The shepherd could not bear to let the sheep off his shoulders *until he got home;* he knew there was no one in the desert that could have any fellowship with him in his joy; there were wolves there, but that was all. He had to wait until he found himself and his precious charge within the quiet walls of his happy home, and then came the outburst of real joy. There was neither enemy nor evil current, nothing to interrupt the hallowed scene in which the heart of the shepherd rejoiced, in fellowship with his friends, over the sheep, for the salvation of which he had toiled so hard.

A WORD ON CHRISTIAN INTERCOURSE.

1 Corinthians x. 31.

It is most needful, when about to offer a word of admonition, to set forth the proper ground on which such a word can be received. The New Testament abounds in admonition, warning, and exhortation; but it clearly lays down the truth as to the position in which the believer is set, before ever he is called to listen to such things; and unless we understand and practically enter into that position, an admonition or a precept may lead to a spirit of legalism or bondage.

Now, as to the position of the believer, as set forth in the Scriptures of the New Testament, it is one of the *most* complete—justification and acceptance. "Justified from *all* things," "*complete* in Him who is the head of all principality and power," "accepted in the Beloved."

These are some of the expressions used by the Holy Spirit to set forth the believer's position before God—a position founded on the accomplished work of Christ, with which, it is needless to say he has nothing whatever to do. God's grace has assigned it to him; the blood of Christ has fitted him to occupy it; and the operation of the Spirit has led him into the understanding and enjoyment of it. His being in it, therefore, is the fruit of the combined action of THE DIVINE THREE IN ONE; nor can aught in him ever interfere with that combined action. The believer's justification, completeness, and acceptance, are as independent of himself and everything in him as is the position of the sun in the heavens. There it is; but who set it there? God. There and thus the believer is; but who set him there? God. Hence one is as independent of him as the other, for both alike are founded on what God is.

It is well to see this—well to have a perfectly unclouded view of what we are, and where we are—well to be led to pause in view of the actings of Divine grace on our behalf—well to allow God to do with us as He will, to make us what He will, and set us where He will; assured, as we may well be, that all is to His infinite glory and praise. We may think it all too good to be true: and too good it would assuredly be, were its truth in any wise dependent upon us; but not when its truth depends entirely on God. It might be too good for us to get; but not too good for God to give. This makes all the difference. When God gives, He gives like Himself. The blessedness of the gift must depend upon the giver. He GIVES perfect justification—He GIVES complete acceptance. To whom? To *sinners.* On what ground? On the ground of Christ's accomplished sacrifice. For what purpose? That they might be to the praise of His glory (John xvii. 2; Acts xiii. 39; Rom. v. *passim;* vi. 23; Eph. i. 6; Col. ii. 10; Eph. i. 12).

Hence, therefore, it is clear that no warning, admonition, precept, or exhortation can, in the most remote manner, involve, affect, or interfere with, the believer's position and relationship. So far from this, the very fact of our being addressed in such a way proves, in the clearest manner, God's gracious recognition of our relationship. If God gives me a command, the fact of His doing so proves that He recognizes in me a principle of life and power, whereby I can both hear and obey. He would not call upon one "dead in trespasses and sins" to do anything. His command to such an one is to receive, as a free gift, eternal life in His Son Jesus Christ. But when one has gotten this life, is born again, has entered into an eternal relationship, based upon redemption, then, and not until then, is he addressed in the language of warning and exhortation; and on his due observance of such language depends much of his present blessing, comfort, and usefulness.

We are prone to confound two things, which differ very materially; namely, our eternal relationship to God as His children, and our present responsibility to Christ as His servants and witnesses. The former is the result of the action of the Divine will and power; as we read in James, "Of His own will begat He us by the word of truth, that we might be a kind of first-fruits of His creatures." The latter, on the contrary, is a thing devolving upon us daily, and calling for much holy diligence in the prayerful study of the word, and waiting upon God. Many of us fail in answering our responsibility to Christ, in manifesting Him in our ways, and in our practical testimony for Him; but this, blessed be God, does not touch our eternal relationship with Him, though it may and does most seriously interfere with our perception and enjoyment as children of God; yea, to talk of one without the other, is to be "deceived by vain words."

This train of thought leads us naturally to the immediate subject of this little paper; namely, Christian Intercourse—a subject of much more importance than might, at first sight, appear. By Christian Intercourse, I do not mean that intercourse which we have on the benches of a meeting-room, or when gathered, on solemn occasions, for worship or edification. The intercourse to which I allude is of a much more commonplace and familiar character; and for that very reason, it needs much more solemn watchfulness, lest in it the enemy should betray us into anything unbecoming the solemnity, purity, and elevation which ought to mark the character and path of those who profess to be members of Christ's holy body and temples of His Holy Spirit.

It is frequently most painful, and deeply humbling, to observe the character of intercourse which prevails now-a-days, amongst those whose professed principles would lead us to look for very different practical results. While marking the intercourse, and hearkening to the conversation which frequently obtains amongst professing Christians of the present day, one feels disposed to ask, Is it possible that these people really believe what they profess? Do they believe that they are "dead and risen with Christ"—that their calling is a heavenly one—that they are part of Christ's body—that they are crucified with Christ—that they are not in the flesh, but in the Spirit—that they are pilgrims and strangers—that they are waiting for God's Son from heaven? It may be, that all these weighty principles are items in the creed to which they have given a nominal assent: but it is morally impossible that their hearts can be affected by them. How could a heart, really under the power of such stupendous truths, take pleasure, or even take part, in vain, frivolous, empty talk—talk about people and their circumstances, with whom, and with which, they have nothing whatever to do—talk about every passing trifle of the day? Could a heart full of Christ be thus occupied? It is as impossible as that noon could intermingle with midnight. Yet professing Christians, when they meet in the drawing-room, at the dinner-table, and at their tea-parties, are, alas! too often found thus occupied.

Nor is it only in our intercourse with our fellow Christians that we forget ourselves, or rather forget the Lord; but also in our intercourse with the world. How often, when we meet with unconverted people, do we slip into the current of their thoughts, and find a theme in common with them! Sometimes this is mourned over, sometimes it is defended, and the defence is founded upon an erroneous view of the apostle's expression, "I am made all things to all." This, surely, does not mean that he entered into the folly and nonsense of worldly men. By no means. This would be to assert entirely too much. What then does the expression mean? It means, that *Paul denied himself amongst all classes of men, in order that he might "by all means save some."* His object was to bring sinners to Christ, and not to please himself by entering into their vain and foolish habits of conversation.

Let us look at the Master Himself, our great Exemplar, and inquire how did He carry Himself toward the men of this world? Did He ever find an object in common with them? Never. He was always feeding upon and filled with one object, and of that object He spoke. He ever sought to lead the thoughts of men to God. This, my beloved reader, should be our object too. Whenever, or wherever we meet men, we should lead them to think of Christ; and if we do not find an open door for that, we should not certainly suffer ourselves to be carried into the current of their thoughts. If we have business to transact with men, we must transact it; but we should not have any fellowship with them in their habits of thought or conversation, because our Master never had; and if we diverge from His path as to this, we shall soon sink into a low and unsanctified tone of spirit. We shall be as "salt that has lost its saltness," and thus be "good for nothing."

I cannot doubt but that much of that lack of deep, settled, habitual peace, of which so many complain, is very justly traceable to the light and trifling habits of conversation in which they indulge; to their reading of newspapers and other light works. Such things must grieve the Holy Spirit; and if the Holy Spirit is grieved, Christ cannot be enjoyed; for it is the Spirit alone who, by the written word, ministers Christ to the soul.

I do not mean to deny that very many feel this lack of peace who do not engage in such things. By no means; but I say that these things must, necessarily, be productive of much serious injury to our spiritual health, and must superinduce a sickly condition of soul, which is most dishonouring to Christ.

It may be, that many who have long been accustomed to high teaching, will turn away from such plain, practical principles as these; but we must expect this. It will be pronounced legalism; and the writer may be accused of seeking to bring people into a sort of bondage, and of casting them upon themselves. I can only say, God forbid. I trust the opening statements of this paper will furnish a very decisive answer to such an accusation. If it be legalism to direct attention to the matter of conversation, then is it the legalism of the Epistle to the Ephesians; for there we find, that "foolish talking and jesting" are amongst the things which are not to be "once named among us, as becometh saints."* Again, we read,

* The word which is rendered "jesting," takes in what is commonly called, "wit," "humour," "punning," "*repartee*," and such-like. It is well to remember this. The word "jesting" would let a great deal pass which should come under the edge of the original word, which is a compound of two Greek words, signifying "to turn well."

"Let your conversation be always with grace, seasoned with salt." These are plain statements of Scripture—statements, moreover, found in immediate connection with some of the most elevated doctrines of inspiration; and it will be found, that where those plain statements are not allowed their full weight on the conscience, the higher truths are not enjoyed. I can neither enjoy nor walk worthy of my "high vocation," if I am indulging in "foolish talking and jesting."

I quite admit the need of carefully avoiding all affected sanctimoniousness, or fleshly restraint. The sanctimoniousness of nature is fully as bad as its levity, if not worse. But why exhibit either the one or the other? The gospel gives us something far better. Instead of affected sanctimoniousness, the gospel gives us real sanctity; and, instead of levity, it gives us holy cheerfulness. There is no need to *affect* anything, for if I am feeding upon Christ, all is reality, without any effort. The moment there is effort, it is all perfect weakness. If I say I must talk about Christ, it becomes terrible bondage, and I exhibit my own weakness and folly; but if my soul is in communion, all is natural and easy: for "out of the abundance of the heart the mouth speaks." It is said of a certain little insect, that it always exhibits the colour of the leaf on which it feeds. So is it exactly with the Christian. It is very easy to tell what he is feeding upon.

But it may be said by some, that "we cannot

be always talking about Christ." I reply, that just in proportion as we are led by an ungrieved Spirit, will all our thoughts and words be occupied about Christ. We, if we are children of God, will be occupied with Him throughout eternity; and why not now? We are as really separated from the world *now*, as we shall be *then*; but we do not walk in the Spirit.

It is quite true, that in entering into the matter of a Christian's habit of conversation, one is taking low ground; but, then, it is needful ground. It would be much happier to keep on the high ground; but, alas! we fail in this; and it is a mercy that Scripture and the Spirit of God meet us in our failure. Scripture tells us we are "seated in heavenly places with Christ;" and it tells us also not "to steal." It may be said that it is low ground to talk to heavenly men about stealing; yet it is Scripture ground; and that is enough for us. The Spirit of God knew that it was not sufficient to tell us that we are seated *in heaven*; He also tells us how to conduct ourselves *on earth*; and our experience of the former will be evidenced by our exhibition of the latter. The walk *here* proves how I enter into my place *there*.

Hence, I may find in the Christian's walk a very legitimate ground on which to deal with him about the actual condition of his soul before God. If his walk is low, carnal, and worldly, it must be evident that he is not realizing his high and holy position as a member of Christ's body and a temple of God.

Wherefore, to all who are prone to indulge in habits of light and trifling conversation, I would affectionately but solemnly say, look well to the general state of your spiritual health. Bad symptoms show themselves—certain evidences of a disease working within—a disease, it may be, more or less affecting the very springs of vitality. Beware how you allow this disease to make progress. Betake yourself at once to the Physician, and partake of His precious balm. Your whole spiritual constitution may be deranged, and nothing can restore its tone, save the healing virtues of what He has to give you.

A fresh view of the excellency, preciousness, and beauty of Christ is the only thing to lift the soul up out of a low condition. All our barrenness and poverty arises from our having let slip Christ. It is not that He has let us slip. No; blessed be His name, this cannot be. But, practically, we have let Him slip, and, as a consequence, our tone has become so low, that it is at times difficult to recognize anything of the Christian in us but the mere name. We have stopped short in our practical career. We have not entered, as we should, into the meaning of Christ's "cup and baptism;" we have failed in seeking fellowship with Him in His sufferings, death, and resurrection. We have sought the result of all these, as wrought out in Him; but we have not entered experimentally into them, and hence our melancholy decline, from which nothing can recover us, but getting more into the fulness of Christ.

JEHOSHAPHAT: A WORD ON WORLD-BORDERING.

"Come out from among them, and be ye separate."

In tracing the inspired record of the houses of Israel and Judah, from the period of their separation under Rehoboam, we can, without difficulty, recognise the marked distinction between them. The line of kings from Jeroboam to Hoshea, presents only a dark and sorrowful catalogue of evil-doers in the sight of the Lord; we look in vain for an exception. Even Jehu, who manifested so much zeal and energy in the abolition of idolatry, proved, in the sequel, that his heart was far from being right with God. In fact, a dark cloud of idolatry seems to have settled upon the whole house of Israel, until they were carried away beyond Babylon and scattered amongst the Gentiles.

Not so, however, with Judah. Here we find some happy exceptions—some pleasant rays from that lamp which the Lord so graciously granted in Jerusalem, for David His servant's sake. The soul is refreshed by the history of such men as

Josiah, Asa, Joash, and Hezekiah—men whose hearts were devoted to the service of the sanctuary, and who, therefore, exerted a holy influence on their times.

It is on the narrative of one of these blessed exceptions that I desire to dwell for a little, trusting the Lord to give instruction and profit in so doing.

Jehoshaphat, king of Judah, is introduced to our notice in 2 Chronicles xvii. In this chapter we find God, in His grace, establishing His servant in the kingdom, and the people of God acknowledging him therein. Jehoshaphat's first act was to "strengthen himself against Israel." This is worthy of notice. Israel and Israel's king were ever a snare to the heart of Jehoshaphat. But, in the opening of his course, in the season of his early freshness, he was able to fortify his kingdom against the power of Israel. Now, one frequently observes this in the history of Christians; the evils which in after-life prove their greatest snares, are those against which there is the greatest watchfulness at first. Most happy is it, when the spirit of watchfulness increases with our increasing knowledge of the tendencies and capabilities of our hearts. But this, alas! is not always the way—on the contrary, how frequently do we find Christians of some years' standing indulging in things which, at the first, their consciences would have shrunk from. This may seem to be but a growing out of a legal spirit; but should it not rather be viewed as a growing out of a tender and sensitive conscience? It would be sad, if the result of more enlarged views were to be a careless spirit or a seared conscience, or if high principles of truth did but tend to render those who were once self-denying and separated, self-indulgent, careless, and worldly! But it is not so. To grow in the knowledge of truth, is to grow in the knowledge of God; and to grow in the knowledge of God, is to grow in practical holiness. The conscience that can let pass, without reproof, things from which it would formerly have shrunk, is, it is much to be feared, instead of being under the action of the truth of God, under the hardening influence of the deceitfulness of sin.

The whole scene presented to us (chap. xvii.) is full of interest. Jehoshaphat not only retains the conquests of Asa, his father, but goes on to extend, by his personal exertions, the interests of his kingdom. All is well ordered. "The Lord was with Jehoshaphat, because he walked in *the first ways* of his father David, and sought not unto Baalim; but sought to the Lord God of his father, and walked in His commandments, and not after the doings of Israel. Therefore the Lord established the kingdom in his hand; and all Judah brought to Jehoshaphat presents; and he had riches and honour in abundance. And his heart was lifted up in the ways of the Lord: moreover, he took away the high places and groves out of

Israel." Here was the true secret of his prosperity: "His heart was lifted up in the ways of the Lord." When the heart is *thus* lifted up, everything goes well.

In chapter xviii., however, we have a very different state of things. Jehoshaphat's prosperity is used by the devil as a snare for him. "Jehoshaphat had riches and honour in abundance, and *joined affinity with Ahab.*" We have already observed Jehoshaphat fortifying his *kingdom;* but the enemy comes upon him in a way for which Jehoshaphat does not seem to have prepared himself; he does not attack his *kingdom,* he attacks his *heart.* He comes not as the lion, but as the serpent. Ahab's "sheep and oxen" are found more suitable and effectual than Ahab's men of war. Had Ahab declared war against Jehoshaphat, it would only have cast him upon the Lord; but he does not. Jehoshaphat's kingdom is fortified against Ahab's hostilities; but his heart lies open to Ahab's allurements. This is truly solemn! We often make a great effort against evil in one shape, while we are allowing it to get in upon us in another. Jehoshaphat had at first strengthened himself against Israel, but now he joins affinity with Israel's king. And why? Had any change for the better taken place? Had Ahab's heart become more tender towards the Lord? By no means. *He* was still the same, but Jehoshaphat's conscience had lost much of its early tenderness and sensitiveness; he had come near to the evil, and tampered with it; he had touched the pitch and was defiled by it. "He joined affinity with Ahab." Here was the evil—an evil which, however slow in its operation, would certainly produce its own fruit, sooner or later. "He that soweth to his flesh, shall of the flesh reap corruption" (Gal. vi. 8). The truth of this must inevitably be realized. Grace may triumph in the forgiveness of sin, but the legitimate fruit will spring forth in due time. The Lord put away David's sin, in the matter of Uriah but the child died, and Absalom rose in rebellion. So it will ever be: if we sow to the flesh, we must reap corruption; the flesh can produce nought else.

In Jehoshaphat's case, it was not until *after-years* that the results of his false step began to show themselves: "And after certain years he went down to Ahab to Samaria; and Ahab killed sheep and oxen for him in abundance, and for the people he had with him, and persuaded him to go with him to Ramoth-gilead." Satan knows his ground; he knows where the seed of evil has taken root; he knows the heart that is prepared to respond to his temptation; he knew that the "affinity" into which the king of Judah had entered with the king of Israel, had prepared him for further steps in a downward course. When a Christian enters into connection with the world, he lays himself open to be "*persuaded*" by the world, to enter upon an *un*christian course of action. David took Ziklag from Achish (1 Sam. xxvii. 6), and the next step was to join Achish against Israel (1 Sam. xxviii. 1). The world will never give anything to a child of God without making large demands in return. When the king of Judah had allowed Ahab to kill sheep and oxen for him, he would have found it difficult not to meet Ahab's desire in reference to Ramoth-gilead. The safest way, therefore, is to be no debtor to the world. Jehoshaphat should have had nothing whatever to do with Ahab; he should have kept himself pure. The Lord was not with Ahab, and though it might seem a desirable thing to recover one of the cities of refuge out of the hand of the enemy, yet Jehoshaphat should have known that he was not to do evil that good might come. If we join with the world in its schemes, we must expect to be identified with it in its convulsions.

Ramoth-gilead had been, of old, assigned as a city of refuge for the slayer (Deut. iv. 43), and to recover this city from the king of Syria, was the object of Ahab's expedition. But, behind this, we can detect the snare of the enemy, who cared little about the city, provided he could thereby betray a child of God from the path of purity and separation. The devil has always found religious and benevolent objects most effectual in their influence upon the people of God. He does not come, at first, with something openly ungodly; he does not tempt a believer to join the world for some wicked design, because he knows that the sensitive conscience would shrink from such a thing; his way is rather to present, in the distance, some desirable object, to cover his schemes with the cloak of religion or benevolence, and thus ensnare. There is, however, one truth which would, if realized, effectually deliver the Christian from all connection with the men of this world. The apostle, by the Holy Ghost, teaches us that unbelievers are "unto *every* good work reprobate" (Tit. i. 16). This is enough for an obedient soul We must not join with those who are so represented. It matters not what they propose—be it a work of benevolence, or a work of religion—Scripture tells us they are reprobate—yes, "reprobate," though they profess that they know God. This should be sufficient. God cannot accept of, or acknowledge, the works or offerings of those whose hearts are far from Him; nor should the Church mingle with such, even though it be for the accomplishment of desirable ends. "Keep thyself pure," is a valuable admonition for us all. "To obey is better than sacrifice, and to hearken than the fat of rams!" It would have been infinitely better and more acceptable for Jehoshaphat to have kept himself pure from all contact with Ahab's defilement, than to have recovered Ramoth from the Syrians, even had he succeeded in doing so.

However, he had to learn this by painful experience. And thus it is that most of us learn our lessons. We may *speak* much of certain points of truth, while we know but little of having learnt them experimentally. When Jehoshaphat, at the commencement of his career, strengthened himself against Israel, he had little idea of the way in which he would afterwards be ensnared by the very worst of Israelites. The only effectual safeguard against evil, is to be in communion with God about it. When we look at evil in the light of the holiness of God, we not only look at the *act*, but at the *principle;* and if the principle be unsound, no matter what the result may be, we should have nothing to do with it. But to deal thus with evil requires much exercise of soul before God—much spirituality—much self-judgment—much prayer and watchfulness. The Lord grant us these, and also more tenderness and godly sensitiveness of conscience.

We have no idea of the sad consequences of a mistake on the part of a child of God. It is not always that the full results appear to us; but the enemy takes care to make his own use of the matter—not in injury done to the one who makes the mistake merely, but to others, who witness and are influenced by it. Jehoshaphat did not only fall into the snare himself; but he led others in also. "I am as thou art," said he; and further, "my people as thy people." What miserably low ground for a man of God to take! and what a place to put the people of God into! "*I am as thou art.*" Thus spake Jehoshaphat, and well was it for him that his words were not verified throughout. God did not judge of *him* as He judged of *Ahab;* here was his real security, even in the midst of the terrible consequences of his unguarded conduct. He was not as Ahab in the close of his career, though he had joined affinity with him for the purpose of carrying out his plans—he was not as Ahab, when Ahab was pierced by an arrow—he was not as Ahab, when the dogs licked Ahab's blood. The Lord had made him to differ.

But we should remember, that when the Christian joins with the world, for any purpose whatsoever, whether of religion or of benevolence, he is just saying (as Jehoshaphat said to Ahab), "I am as thou art." Let the Christian reader ask his own heart, Is this right? Is he prepared to say this? It will not do to say, "We are not to judge others." Jehoshaphat ought to have judged, as is manifest from the language of Jehu the prophet, when he met him on his return from Ramoth: "Shouldest thou help the ungodly, and love them that hate the Lord?" How was he to know who was ungodly, or who hated the Lord, if he did not exercise judgment? We have certainly no right to judge those that are without, but we are bound to exercise judgment as to those with whom we enter into fellowship. Nor does this in the least involve, of necessity, the idea of one's own personal superiority in any one particular. No, it is not, "Stand by thyself, *I* am holier than *thou;*" but, "I must stand apart, because *God is holy.*" This is the true principle. It is upon the ground of what God is (not of what we are) that we separate from known evil. "Be *ye* holy, for *I* am holy."

Jehoshaphat, however, failed to maintain this separation; and, as has already been remarked, in failing himself, led others into failure. In this we may learn a most solemn lesson. Jehoshaphat had, we may suppose, gained very considerable influence over the hearts of the people, by his previous devotedness; he had established himself in their confidence and affections; and, to a certain extent, rightly so. It is right that those who walk devotedly should be loved and confided in; but then we must watch, most jealously, against the dangerous tendency of mere personal influence. No one, save a man of extensive influence, could have said, "My people are as thy people:" he might have said, "I am as thou art," but no more. His extensive influence, when used out of communion, only made him a more efficient instrument of evil. Satan knew this; he knew his mark; he did not fasten on an ordinary man of Judah, but on the most prominent and influential man he could find, well knowing that if he could only succeed in drawing him aside, others would follow in his train.

Nor was he mistaken. Many would, no doubt, say, "What harm can there be in joining Ahab's expedition? Surely, if there were anything wrong in it, such a good man as king Jehoshaphat would not engage in it; so long as we see *him* there, *we* may make our minds easy about the matter." But if this were not the language of some in Jehoshaphat's day, it certainly is of many in our own; how often do we hear Christians say, "How can such and such things be wrong, when we see such good men in connection with them, or engaging in them?" Now, all that can be said of such reasoning is, that it is thoroughly false; it is beginning quite at the wrong end. We are responsible to God to act upon principle, let others do as they may. We should be able, through grace, humbly, yet decidedly, to render a sound and intelligent reason for whatever course of action we may adopt, without any reference to the conduct of others. Moreover, we know full well, that good men go astray and do wrong things; they are not, therefore, nor can they be, our guides. "To his own Master he standeth or falleth." A spiritual mind —a conscience enlightened by the word of God—a real sense of personal responsibility, together with honesty of purpose, are what we specially need. If we lack these, our path will be defective.

But, it may be said, there are few, if any, who occupy a position in which their conduct could exert such an extensive influence as that of king Jehoshaphat. To meet this, it may be needful to dwell a little upon a truth sadly neglected in the present day, namely, that of *the unity of the body of Christ, and the consequent effect which the conduct of each member, however obscure, must produce upon the whole body.*

The great doctrine of the unity of the Church upon earth is, it is to be feared, feebly apprehended and feebly carried out, even by the most spiritually minded and intelligent of the Lord's people. The reason of this is very apparent; the doctrine is viewed, rather in the light of the Church's present condition, than of her condition as presented in the New Testament; and this being so, the unity never can be understood. If we simply take Scripture for our guide, we shall have no difficulty about it. There we read, "If *one* member suffer, *all* the members suffer with it." This principle did not hold good in the days of king Jehoshaphat, because the body of Christ, properly so called, had no actual existence; all the members of it were written in God's book, but "as yet, there was none of them"—they existed in the purpose of God, but that purpose had not been actualized. Hence, though so many were led astray by the influence of Jehoshaphat, it was not, by any means, on the principle stated in the above passage—it was not all suffering from the act of one, because they were one body, but many being led astray by one, because they followed his example. The distinction is very important. There is no member of the Church, how obscure soever, whose path and conduct do not affect, in some measure, all the members. "By one Spirit are we all baptized into one body, whether we be Jews or Gentiles, whether we be bond or free; and have been all made to drink into one Spirit." Hence, if a Christian be walking loosely or carelessly—if he be out of communion—if he fail in prayer, in watchfulness, or in self-judgment, he is really injuring the whole body; and, on the contrary, when he is walking in spiritual health and vigour, he is promoting the blessing and interest of all.

It was not without a struggle that Jehoshaphat yielded to the solicitations of Ahab. The working of conscience is observable in the words, "Inquire, I pray thee, at the word of the Lord, to-day." But, ah! how futile was prayer for guidance, when he had already said, "I am as thou art, and my people as thy people; and we will be with thee in the war!" It is but solemn mockery to ask for guidance when we have made up our minds; and yet how frequently we do so! How frequently do we decide on a course of action, and then go and ask the Lord about it! All this is wretched! it is only honouring God with the lips, while the heart is in positive rebellion against Him. Instead of getting that guidance, for which we profess to ask, may we not rather expect a lying spirit to be sent forth to us? (Ver. 21).

Ahab was at no loss for counsellors; he speedily "gathered together four hundred prophets," who were ready to counsel him according to his heart's desire: "Go up; for God will deliver it into the king's hand." This was what he wanted. Nor need we marvel at Ahab's being quite satisfied with prophets like these; they suited him well.

But, surely, Jehoshaphat should not have even appeared to acknowledge them to be prophets of the Lord, as he evidently did, by saying, "Is there not here a prophet of the Lord *beside?*" (or, as the margin reads, "yet one more.") Had he been faithful to the Lord, he would at once have denied the right of these false prophets to give counsel. But, alas! he was giving full countenance to the religion of the world, and to these its ministers. He could not bring himself to hurt Ahab's feelings, by dealing faithfully with his prophets. They were all, it would seem, proper men. How dreadful a thing it is to allow ourselves to get into a condition of soul in which we are unable to bear distinct and faithful testimony against the ministers of Satan! "We must," it is said, "be liberal"—"we must not hurt people's feelings,"—"there are good men everywhere." But truth is truth, and we are not to put error for truth, nor truth for error. Nothing but a secret desire to stand well with the world will ever lead to this careless method of dealing with evil. Now, if we want to stand well with the world, let us do it at our own charges, and not at the expense of God's truth. It is often urged. "We must present truth in such an aspect as will attract," when what is really meant is this, that truth is to be made a kind of variable, elastic thing, which can be turned into any shape, or stretched to any length, to suit the tastes and habits of those who would fain put it out of the world altogether.

Truth, however, cannot be thus treated; it can never be made to reduce itself to the level of this world. Those who profess to hold it may seek to use it thus; but it will ever be found the same pure, holy, faithful witness against the world and all its ways; it will speak distinctly, if its voice be not stifled by connection with the practice of its faithless professors. When Jehoshaphat had stooped so low as to acknowledge the false prophets, for the purpose of gratifying Ahab, who could observe any distinct testimony for God? All seemed to sink down to the one common level, and the enemy to have it all his own way; the voice of truth was hushed—the prophets prophesied falsely—God was forgotten. Thus must it ever be. The attempt to accommodate truth to those who are of the world, can only end in complete failure. There can be no accommodation. Let it stand upon its own heavenly height,—let saints stand fully and firmly with it—let them invite sinners up to them, but let them not descend to the low and grovelling pursuits and habits of the world, and thus rob truth, so far as in them lies, of all its edge and power. It is far better to allow the contrast between God's truth and our ways to be fully seen, than to attempt to identify them in appearance, when they really do not agree. We may think to commend truth to the minds of worldly people, by an effort to conform to their ways: but, so far from commending it, we, in reality, expose it to secret contempt and scorn. Jehoshaphat certainly did not further the cause of truth, by conforming to Ahab's ways, or by acknowledging the claims of his false prophets. The man who conforms to the world will be the enemy of Christ, and the enemy of Christ's people. It cannot be otherwise. "The friendship of the world is enmity with God; whosoever therefore will be a friend of the world, is the enemy of God."

How fully was this proved in the case of king Jehoshaphat; he became the friend and companion of Ahab, who hated Micaiah, the servant of God; and, as a consequence, although he did not, himself, positively persecute the righteous witness, yet he did what was as bad; for he sat beside Ahab, and beheld the Lord's prophet first struck, and then committed to prison, simply because he would not tell a lie to please a wicked king, and harmonize with four hundred wicked prophets. What must have been the feelings of Jehoshaphat when he beheld his brother smitten and imprisoned for his faithfulness in testifying against an expedition, in which he himself was engaged? Yet, such was the position into which his connection with Ahab had forced him, that he could not avoid being a witness of these wicked proceedings; yea, and moreover, a partaker of them also. When a man associates himself with the world, he must do so thoroughly; the enemy will not be satisfied with half measures; on the contrary, he will use every effort to force a saint, out of communion, into the most terrible extremes of evil. The beginning of evil is like the letting out of water. Small beginnings lead to fearful results. There is, first, a slight tampering with evil at a distance; then, by degrees, a nearer approach to it; after this, a taking hold of it more firmly; and, finally, a deliberate plunge into it, whence nothing but the most marked interposition of God can rescue. Jehoshaphat "joined affinity with Ahab;" then accepted of his hospitality; after that, was "persuaded" into open association with him; and, finally, took *his* place at the battle of Ramoth-gilead. He had said to Ahab, "I am as thou art," and Ahab takes him at his word; for he says to him, "I will disguise myself, and will go to the battle; but put thou on thy robes." Thus, so completely did Jehoshaphat surrender his personal identity, in the view of the men of the world, that "it came to pass, when the captains of the chariots saw Jehoshaphat, that they said, *It is the king of Israel.*" Terrible position for Jehoshaphat! To find him personating, and thus mistaken for, the worst of Israel's kings, is a sad proof of the danger of associating with the men of the world. Happy was it for Jehoshaphat that the Lord did not take him at his word, when he said to Ahab, "I am as thou art." The Lord knew that Jehoshaphat was not Ahab, though he might personate and be mistaken for him. Grace had made him to differ, and conduct should have *proved* him to be what grace had made him. But, blessed be God, "He knows how to deliver the godly out of temptation," and He graciously delivered His poor servant out of the evil into which he had plunged himself, and in which he would have perished, had not the hand of God been stretched out to rescue him.

"Jehoshaphat cried out, and the Lord helped him; and God moved them to depart from him."*

Here we have the turning point in this stage of Jehoshaphat's life. His eyes were opened to see the position into which he had brought himself; at least, he saw his danger, if he did not apprehend the moral evil of his course. Encompassed by the captains of Syria, he could feel something of what it was to have taken Ahab's place. Happily for him, however, he could look up to the Lord, from the depth of his distress; he could cry out to Him, in the time of his extremity; had it not been thus, the enemy's arrow, lodged deep in his heart, might have told out the sorrowful result of his ungodly association. "Jehoshaphat cried out," and his cry came up before the Lord, whose ear is ever open to hear the cry of such as feel their

* The reader will, doubtless, observe how the inspired writer presents God under two different titles, in the above verse. "*The Lord*," brings out His connection with His distressed servant—His connection in grace; while the expression "*God*," shows out the powerful control which He exercised over the Syrian captains. It is needless to say that this distinction is divinely perfect. As Lord, He deals with His own redeemed people—meeting all their weakness, and supplying all their need; but as God, He holds in His omnipotent hand the hearts of all men, to turn them whithersoever He will. Now we generally find unconverted persons using the expression "God" and not "Lord." They think of Him as one exercising an influence from a distance, rather than as one standing in near relationship. Jehoshaphat knew who it was that "*helped him;*" but the Syrian captains did not know who it was that "*moved them.*"

need. "Peter went out and wept bitterly." The prodigal said, "I will arise and go to my father;" and the father ran to meet him, and fell on his neck, and kissed him. Thus is it, that the blessed God ever meets those who, feeling that they have hewn out for themselves broken cisterns, which can hold no water, return to Him, the fountain of living waters. Would that all who feel that they have in any measure departed from Christ, and slipped into the current of this present world, might find their way back in true humility and contrition of spirit to Him who says, "Behold, I stand at the door, and knock; if any man hear my voice, and open the door, I will come in to him, and will sup with him, and he with me."

How different Ahab's case! He, though carrying in his bosom a mortal wound, propped himself up in his chariot until the evening—fondly desiring to hide his weakness, and accomplish the object of his heart. We find no cry of humility—no tear of penitence—no looking upward. Ah! no; we find not anything but what is in full keeping with his entire course. He died as he had lived, doing evil in the sight of the Lord. How fruitless were his efforts to prop himself up! Death had seized upon him; and though he struggled for a time to keep up an appearance, yet, "about the time of the sun going down, he died." Terrible end! the end of one who had "sold himself to work wickedness!" Who would be the votary of the world? Who, that valued a life of simplicity and purity, would mix himself up with its pursuits and habits? Who, that valued a peaceful and happy termination of his career, would link himself with its destinies?

Dear Christian reader, let us, with the Lord's help, endeavour to shake off the world's influence, and purge ourselves from its ways. We have no idea how insidiously it creeps in upon us. The enemy at first weans from really simple and Christian habits; and by degrees we drop into the current of the world's thoughts. Oh! that we may with more holy jealousy and tenderness of conscience watch against the approach of evil, lest the solemn statement of the prophet should apply to us, "Her Nazarites *were* purer than snow, they *were* whiter than milk, they *were* more ruddy in body than rubies, their polishing *was* of sapphire: (but, such is the sorrowful change, that) their visage *is* blacker than a coal; *they are not known in the streets;* their skin cleaveth to their bones; it is withered, it is become like a stick!"

We shall now look a little at chapter xix. Here we see some blessed results from all that Jehoshaphat had passed through. "He returned to his house in peace to Jerusalem." Happy escape! The Lord's hand had interposed for him, and delivered him from the snare of the fowler, and, we may say, he would no doubt have his heart full of gratitude to Him who had so made him to differ from Ahab, though he had said, "I am as thou art." Ahab had gone down to his grave in shame and degradation, while Jehoshaphat returned to his house in peace. But what a lesson he had learned! How solemn to think of his having been so near the brink of the precipice! Yet the Lord had a controversy with him about what he had done. Though he allowed him to return in peace to Jerusalem, and did not suffer the enemy to hurt him, he would speak to his conscience about his sin, he would bring him aside from the field of battle to deal with him in private. "And Jehu, the son of Hanani the seer, went out to meet him, and said to King Jehoshaphat, Shouldest thou help the ungodly, and love them that hate the Lord? therefore is wrath upon thee from before the Lord." This was a solemn appeal, and it produced its own effect. Jehoshaphat "went out again through the people, from Beersheba to mount Ephraim, and brought them back unto the Lord God of their fathers." "When thou art converted, strengthen thy brethren." Thus did Peter; thus, too, did King Jehoshaphat; and blessed is it, when lapses and failings lead, through the Lord's tender mercy, to such a result. Nothing but divine grace can ever produce this. When, after beholding Jehoshaphat surrounded by the Syrian captains (chap. xviii.), we find him here going out through the length and breadth of the land to instruct his brethren in the fear of the Lord, we can only exclaim, "What hath God wrought!" But he was just the man for such a work. It is one who has felt in his own person the terrible fruits of a careless spirit that can most effectually say, "*Take heed what ye do.*" A restored Peter, who had himself denied the Holy One, was the chosen vessel to go and charge others with having done the same, and to offer them that precious blood which had cleansed his conscience from the guilt of it. So, likewise, the restored Jehoshaphat came from the battle of Ramoth-gilead, to sound in the ears of his brethren, with solemn emphasis, "Take heed what ye do." He that had just escaped from the snare could best tell what it was, and tell how to avoid it.

And mark the special feature in the Lord's character which engaged Jehoshaphat's attention: "There is no iniquity with the Lord our God, *nor respect of persons, nor taking of gifts.*" Now his snare seems to have been the gift of Ahab: "Ahab slew sheep and oxen for him in abundance, and for the people he had with him, and persuaded him to go up with him to Ramoth-gilead." He allowed his heart to be warmed by Ahab's gift, and was thereby the more easily swayed by Ahab's arguments. Just as Peter accepted the compliment of being let into the high-priest's fire, and, being warmed thereby, denied his Lord. We can never canvass, with spiritual coolness, the world's arguments and suggestions, while we are breathing its atmosphere, or accepting its compliments. We must keep outside and independent of it, and thus we shall find ourselves in a better position to reject its proposals, and triumph over its allurements.

But it is instructive to mark how Jehoshaphat, after his restoration, dwells upon that feature in the Divine character from the lack of which he had so grievously failed. Communion with God is the great safeguard against all temptation, for there is no sin to which we are tempted of which we cannot find the opposite in God, and we can only avoid evil by communion with good. This is a very simple, but deeply practical truth. Had Jehoshaphat been in fellowship with God, he could not have sought fellowship with Ahab. And may we not say this is the only Divine way in which to look at the question of worldly association. Let us ask ourselves, Can our association with the world go hand-in-hand with our fellowship with God? This is really the question. It is a miserable thing to ask, May I not partake of all the benefits of the name of Christ, and yet dishonour that name, by mixing myself up with the people of the world, and taking common ground with them? How easily the matter is settled, when we bring it into the Divine presence, and under the searching power of the truth of God: "Shouldest thou help the ungodly, and love them that hate the Lord?" Truth strips off all the false covering which a heart out of communion is wont to throw around things. It is only when *it* casts its unerring beams on our path, that we see things in their true character. Mark the way in which Divine truth exposed the actings of Ahab and Jezebel. Jezebel would fain put a fair cloak on her shocking wickedness: "Arise," said she, "and take possession of the vineyard of Naboth the Jezreelite, which he refused to give thee for money, for Naboth is not alive, but dead." Such was her way of putting the matter; but how did the Lord view it? "Thus saith the Lord, Hast thou killed, and also taken possession?" (in other words, Hast thou committed murder and robbery?) God deals with realities. In His estimation men and things get their proper place and value; there is no gilding, no affectation, no assumption—all is real. Just so was it with Jehoshaphat; his scheme, which might in human estimation be regarded as a religious one, was in the Divine judgment pronounced to be a simple helping of the ungodly, and loving them that hated the Lord. While men might applaud him, "there was wrath upon him from before the Lord."

However, Jehoshaphat had to be thankful for the salutary lesson which his fall had taught him; it had taught him to walk more in the fear of the Lord, and caused him to impress that more upon others also. This was doing not a little. True, it was a sad and painful way to learn; but it is well when we learn even by our falls; it is well when we can tell, even by painful experience, the terrible evil of being mixed up with the world. Would to God we all felt it more! Would that we more walked in the solemn apprehension of the defiling nature of all worldly association, and of our own tendency to be defiled thereby; we should then be more efficient teachers of others; we should be able to say, with somewhat more weight, "Take heed what ye do;" and again, "Deal courageously, and the Lord shall be with the good."

In chapter xx. we find Jehoshaphat in far more healthful circumstances than in chapter xviii. He is here seen under trial from the hand of the enemy: "It came to pass after this also that the children of Moab and the children of Ammon, and with them others beside the Ammonites, came against Jehoshaphat to battle." We are in far less apprehension for Jehoshaphat when we behold him the object of the enemy's hostilities, than when we beheld him the subject of Ahab's kindness and hospitality; and very justly so, for in the one case he is about to be cast simply on the God of Israel, whereas, in the other, he was about to fall into the snare of Satan. The proper place for the man of God is to be in positive opposition to the enemies of the Lord, and not in conjunction with them. We never can count upon divine sympathy or guidance when we join with the enemies of the Lord. Hence we observe what an empty thing it was of Jehoshaphat, to ask counsel of the Lord in a matter which he knew to be wrong. Not so, however, in the scene before us. He is really in earnest when "he sets himself to seek the Lord, and proclaims a fast throughout all Judah." This is real work. There is nothing like trial from the hand of the world for driving the saint into a place of separation from it. When the world smiles we are in danger of being attracted, but when it frowns we are driven away from it into our stronghold, and this is both happy and healthful. Jehoshaphat did not say to a Moabite or an Ammonite, "I am as thou art"—no; he knew well this was not so, for they would not let him think so. And how much better it is to know our true position in reference to the world.

There are three special points in Jehoshaphat's address to the Lord. (Vers. 6—12.)

1st. The greatness of God.

2nd. The oath to Abraham about the land.

3rd. The attempt of the enemy to drive the seed of Abraham out of that land.

The prayer is most precious and instructive—full of divine intelligence. He makes it altogether a question between the God of Abraham and the children of Ammon, Moab, and Mount Seir. This is what faith ever does; and the issue will ever be the same. "They come," says he, "to cast us out of *Thy possession, which Thou hast given us to inherit.*" How simple! *They* would take what *Thou* hast given! This was putting it, as it were, upon God, to maintain His own covenant. "O our God, *wilt Thou not judge them? for we have no might* against this great company that cometh against us; neither know we what to do; but our eyes are upon Thee." Surely we may say, victory was already secured to one who could thus deal with God. And so Jehoshaphat felt. For "when he had consulted with the people, *he appointed singers unto the Lord*, and that should praise the beauty of holiness, as they went out before the army, and to say, Praise the Lord; for His mercy endureth for ever." Nothing but faith could raise a song of praise before even the battle had begun.

"Faith counts the promise sure."

And as it had enabled Abraham to believe that God would put his seed into the possession of Canaan, so it enabled Jehoshaphat to believe that He would keep them therein, and he therefore did not need to wait for victory in order to praise; he already stood in the full results of victory. Faith could say, "Thou *hast guided* them in Thy strength unto Thy holy habitation," though they had but just entered into the wilderness.

But what a strange sight it must have been for the enemies of Jehoshaphat, to see a band of men with musical instruments, instead of weapons, in their hands. It was something of the same principle of warfare as that adopted by Hezekiah afterwards, when he clothed himself in sackcloth instead of armour (Isa. xxxvii. 1).* Yes, it was

* "The proud king of Assyria was at the gates of Jerusalem with a mighty conquering host, and one would naturally expect to find Hezekiah in the midst of his men of war—buckling on his armour—girding on his sword—mounting his chariot; but no; Hezekiah was different from most kings and captains—he had found out a place of strength which was

the same, for both had been trained in the same school, and both fought under the same banner.

quite unknown to Sennacherib—he had discovered a field of battle in which he could conquer, without striking a blow. And mark the armour with which he girds himself: 'And it came to pass, when Hezekiah heard it, that he rent his clothes, and *covered himself with sackcloth*, and went into the house of the Lord.' Here was the armour in which the king of Judah was about to cope with the king of Assyria. Strange armour! The armour of the sanctuary. What would Sennacherib have said had he seen this? He had never met such an antagonist before—he had never come in contact with a man who, instead of covering himself with a coat of mail, would cover himself with sackcloth, and instead of rushing forth into the field of battle in his chariot, would fall upon his knees in the temple. This would have appeared a novel mode of warfare in the eyes of the king of Assyria. He had met the kings of Amath and Arphad, &c.: but if he had, it was upon his own principle, and in his own way; but he had never encountered such an antagonist as Hezekiah. In fact, what gave the latter such uncommon power in this contest, was the feeling that *he* was nothing—that an 'arm of flesh' was of no avail: in a word, that it was just Jehovah or nothing. This is specially seen in the act of spreading the letter before the Lord. Hezekiah was enabled by faith to retire out of the scene, and make it altogether a question between Jehovah and the king of Assyria. It was not Sennacherib and Hezekiah; but Sennacherib and Jehovah. This tells us the meaning of the sackcloth. Hezekiah felt himself to be utterly helpless, and he took the place of helplessness—he tells the Lord that the king of Assyria had reproached *Him*—he calls upon Him to vindicate His own glorious name, feeling assured, that in so doing, He would deliver His people. Mark, then, this wondrous scene. Repair to the sanctuary, and there behold one, poor, weak, solitary man on his knees—pouring out his soul to Him

Would that our warfare with the present age—

who dwelt between the cherubim—no military preparations—no reviewing of troops—the elders of the priests, covered with sackcloth, pass to and fro from Hezekiah to the prophet Isaiah—all is apparent weakness. On the other hand, see a mighty conqueror leading on a numerous army flushed with victory, eager for spoil. Surely one might say, speaking after the manner of men, all is over with Hezekiah and Jerusalem—surely Sennacherib and his proud host will swallow up, in a moment, such a feeble band! And observe, further, the ground which Sennacherib takes in all this (Isa. xxxvi. 4–7). Here we observe that Sennacherib makes the very reformation which Hezekiah had effected a ground of reproach; thus leaving him, as he vainly thought, no resting-place or foundation for his confidence. Again he says, 'Am I come up without the Lord against this land to destroy it? *The Lord said unto me, Go up against this land and destroy it*' (ver. 10). This was indeed putting Hezekiah's faith to the test—faith must pass through the furnace—it will not do to *say* that we trust in the Lord, we must *prove* that we do, and that too when everything, apparently, is against us. How, then, does Hezekiah meet all these lofty words? In the silent dignity of faith. 'The king's commandment was, saying, Answer him not' (ver. 21). Such was the king's bearing in the eyes of the people; yea, rather, such is ever the bearing of faith—calm—self-possessed—dignified, in the presence of man; while, at the same time, ready to sink into the very dust in self-abasement in the presence of God. The man of faith can say to his fellow, 'Stand still, and see the salvation of God;' and, at the same moment, send up to God the cry of conscious weakness. (See Exodus xiv. 13–15.) So it was with the king of Judah at this solemn and trying crisis. Hearken to him while, in the retirement of the sanctuary, shut in with God, he pours out the anxieties of his soul in the ear of One who was willing to hear and ready to help (chap. xxxvii. 15–20)."—*Practical Reflections on the Life and Times of Hezekiah.*

with its habits, manners, and maxims, were more conducted on the same principle. "Above all, taking the shield of faith, wherewith ye shall be able to quench all the fiery darts of the wicked one."

What a contrast between Jehoshaphat personating Ahab at Ramoth-gilead, and standing with the Lord against his enemies, the Moabites! Yes; what a contrast, in every particular! His mode of seeking help and guidance of the Lord was different—his mode of proceeding to battle was different; and oh! how different, too, the end! Instead of being well-nigh overwhelmed by the enemy, and crying out in the depth of his distress and danger, we find him joining in a loud chorus of praise to the God of his fathers, who had given him a victory, without his striking a blow—who had made his enemies destroy one another, and who had graciously conducted him from the dark valley of Achor into the valley of Berachah. Blessed contrast! May it lead us to seek a more decided path of separation and of abiding dependence on the Lord's grace and faithfulness. The valley of Berachah, or praise, is ever the place into which the Spirit of God would conduct; but He cannot lead us thither when we join ourselves with the "Ahabs" of this world, for the purpose of carrying out their schemes. The word is, "Come out from among them, and be ye separate, saith the Lord, and touch not the unclean thing, and I will receive you, and will be a Father unto you, and ye shall be my sons and daughters, saith the Lord Almighty" (2 Cor. vi. 17, 18).

It is wonderful how worldliness hinders, yea, rather, destroys, a spirit of praise; it is positively hostile to such a spirit, and, if indulged in, it will either lead to deep anguish of soul, or to the most thorough and open abandonment of all semblance of godliness. In Jehoshaphat's case, it was, happily, the former. He was humbled, restored, and led into larger blessedness.

But it would be sad, indeed, were any one to plunge into worldliness with the hope that it might lead to an issue similar to that of Jehoshaphat. Vain, presumptuous hope! Sinful expectation! Who that valued a pure, calm, and peaceful walk, could for a moment entertain it? "The Lord knoweth how to deliver the godly out of temptation," but shall we, on that account, go and deliberately plunge ourselves into it? God forbid.

Yet, ah! who can sound the depths of the human heart—its profound, malignant depths? Who can disentangle its complicated mazes? Could any one imagine that Jehoshaphat would again, after such solemn lessons, join himself with the ungodly, to further their ambitious, or rather, their avaricious schemes? No one could imagine it, save one who had learned something of his own heart. Yet so he did. "He joined himself with Ahaziah king of Israel, who did very wickedly: and he joined himself with him to make ships to go to Tarshish: and they made the ships in Ezion-gaber. Then Eliezer the son of Dodavah of Mareshah prophesied against Jehoshaphat, saying, Because thou hast joined thyself with Ahaziah, the Lord hath broken thy works. And the ships were broken, and they were not able to go to Tarshish" (vers. 35—37). What is man! A poor, stumbling, failing, halting creature, ever rushing into some new folly or evil. Jehoshaphat had, as it were, but just recovered from the effects of his association with Ahab, and he forthwith joins himself with Ahaziah. He had with difficulty, or rather through the special and most gracious interference of the Lord, escaped from the arrows of the Syrians, and again we find him in league with the kings of Israel and Edom, to fight against the Moabites.

Such was Jehoshaphat—such his extraordinary course. There were some "good things found in him," but his snare was worldly association, and the lesson which we learn from the consideration of his history is to beware of that evil. Yes; we would need to have sounded in our ears, with ceaseless solemnity, the words, "COME OUT, AND BE SEPARATE." We cannot touch pitch and not be defiled thereby, and we cannot, by any possibility, mix ourselves up with the world, and allow ourselves to be governed by its maxims and principles, without suffering in our own souls, and marring our testimony.

I would only remark, in conclusion, that it seems like a relief to the spirit to read the words, "Jehoshaphat slept with his fathers" (chap. xxi. 1), as we feel assured that he has at last got beyond the reach of the enemy's snares and devices; and, further, that he comes under the Spirit's benediction, "Blessed are the dead which die in the Lord; for they rest from their labours,"—yes, and rest from their conflicts, snares, and temptations also.

THE TRUE NATURE OF THE SABBATH, THE LAW, AND THE CHRISTIAN MINISTRY.

In resuming our lectures for the winter months, we feel called upon to offer a few words of explanation to all such as may be desirous of knowing something of the doctrines held by those persons who stand connected, in any measure, with this service.

We feel that such persons have a claim upon us, to which we ought to respond, not for the purpose of vindicating ourselves, but simply to guard the truth against misrepresentation, and to remove, so far as in us lies, a stumbling-block out of the way of honest inquirers.

"Charity thinketh no evil;" and hence we shall not allow ourselves to think that any one could wilfully misrepresent our opinions; but it is a well-known fact that the most extravagant ideas are current in reference to these opinions; and while we can leave all those who have given currency to such ideas, to Him before whose judgment-seat all must stand (2 Cor. v. 10), we, at the same time, deem ourselves responsible "to give a reason of the hope that is in us," and of the ground which we occupy, "with meekness and fear" (1 Pet. iii. 15), in order to meet those who may be scared away from the consideration of truth, by the fact that monstrous errors are attributed to the persons who profess to hold and teach that truth. We all know how prone we are to receive an opinion ready made to our hand, rather than take the trouble of investigating matters for ourselves, and comparing what is put before us, not with our own or other's preconceived judgment or opinion, but with the word of God.

The Bereans were counted "more noble than those in Thessalonica," not because they consulted the decrees or traditions of the elders, but because "they searched the Scriptures daily, whether those things were so" (Acts xvii. 11). Now, this is precisely what we want the reader to do. We want him to imitate the "noble" conduct of the Bereans. We want him to "search the Scriptures" with an unbiassed mind. We want him to form his convictions, not amid the darkness of misrepresentation and prejudice, but amid the pure and hallowed light which the page of inspiration sheds around him. We would affectionately entreat him to watch against a disposition to think people in error, merely because their position differs from his own. Let him seek for a dispassionate judgment, a calm, well-adjusted mind, a liberal spirit. In this way, if he cannot agree with people, he will, at least, refrain from hard feelings and hard words, neither of which can possibly serve any desirable end, either as regards himself or others. To ascertain truth is the object of every judicious and reflecting mind, and this object should ever be pursued with a spirit freed from the defiling and withering influences of a narrow and demoralizing bigotry.

We shall now proceed with the special subject of these pages.

There are three important points in reference to which we are entirely misrepresented, namely, the Sabbath, the Law, and the Christian Ministry.

And first, as to the SABBATH. If it were merely a question of the observance or non-observance of a day, it might be easily disposed of, inasmuch as the apostle teaches us in Romans xiv. 5, 6, and also in Colossians ii. 16, that such things are not to be made a ground of judgment. But seeing there is a great principle involved in the Sabbath question, we deem it to be of the very last importance to place it upon a clear and scriptural basis. We shall quote the fourth commandment at full length. "Remember the Sabbath-day to keep it holy. Six days shalt thou labour and do all thy work: but the seventh day is the Sabbath of the Lord thy God: in it thou shalt not do any work, thou, nor thy son, nor thy daughter, thy man-servant, nor thy maid-servant, nor thy cattle, nor the stranger that is within thy gates: for in six days the Lord made heaven and earth, the sea and all that in them is, and rested the seventh day; wherefore the Lord blessed the seventh day and hallowed it" (Exod. xx. 8–11). This same law is repeated in Exodus xxxi. 12–17. And, in pursuance thereof, we find, in Numbers xv., a man stoned for gathering sticks on the Sabbath-day. All this is plain and absolute enough. Man has no right to alter God's law in reference to the Sabbath, no more than he has to alter it in reference to murder, adultery, or theft. This, we presume, will not be called in question. The entire body of Old Testament Scripture fixes the seventh day as the Sabbath; and the fourth commandment lays down the mode in which that Sabbath was to be observed. Now where, we ask, is this precedent followed? Where is this command obeyed? Is it not plain that the professing Church neither keeps the right day as the Sabbath, nor does she keep it after the Scripture mode? The commandments of God are made of none effect by human traditions, and the glorious truths which hang around "the Lord's day" are lost sight of. The Jew is robbed of his distinctive day, and all the privileges therewith connected, which are only suspended for the present, while judicial blindness hangs over that loved and interesting, though now judged and scattered, people. And, furthermore, the Church is robbed of her distinctive day and all the glories therewith connected, which, if really understood, would have the effect of lifting her above earthly things into the sphere which properly belongs to her as linked by faith to her glorified Head in heaven. In result, we have neither pure Judaism nor pure Christianity, but an anomalous system arising out of an utterly unscriptural combination of the two.

However, we desire to refrain from all attempt at developing the deeply spiritual doctrine involved in this great question, and confine ourselves to the plain teaching of Scripture on the subject; and, in so doing, we maintain that if the professing Church quotes the fourth commandment and parallel Scriptures, in defence of keeping the Sabbath, then it is evident, that, in almost every case, the law is entirely set aside. Observe, the word is, "Thou shalt not do *any* work." This ought to be perfectly binding on all who take the Jewish ground. There is no room here for introducing what we deem to be "works of necessity," we may think it necessary to kindle fires, to make servants harness our horses and drive us hither and thither, but the law is stern and absolute, severe and unbending. It will not, it cannot, lower its standard to suit our convenience or accommodate itself to our thoughts. The mandate is, "Thou shalt not do *any* work," and that, moreover, on "the seventh day," which answers to our Saturday. We ask for a single passage of Scripture in which the day is changed, or in which the strict observance of the day is, in the smallest degree, relaxed.

We request the reader of these lines to pause and search out this matter thoroughly, in the light of Scripture. Let him not be scared as by some terrible bugbear, but let him, in true Berean nobility of spirit, "search the Scriptures." By so doing, he will find that, from the second chapter of Genesis, down to the very last passage in which the Sabbath is named, it means the *seventh* day and none other; and, further, that there is not so much as a shadow of Divine authority for altering the mode of observing that day. Law is law; and, if we are under the law, we are bound to keep it, or else be cursed; for "it is written, Cursed is every one that continueth not in all things which are written in the book of the law to do them" (Deut. xxvii. 26; Gal. iii. 10).

But it will be said, "We are not under the Mosaic law; we are the subjects of the Christian economy." Granted—most fully, freely, and thankfully granted. All true Christians are, according to the teaching of Romans vii. and viii. and Galations iii. and iv. the happy and privileged subjects of the Christian dispensation. But, if so, what is the day which specially characterises that dispensation? Not "the seventh day," but "the first day of the week"—"THE LORD'S-DAY." This is, pre-eminently, the Christian's day. Let him observe this day, with all the sanctity, the sacred reverence, the hallowed retirement, the elevated tone, of which his new nature is capable. We believe the Christian's retirement from all secular things cannot possibly be too profound on the Lord's-day. The idea of any one calling himself a Christian, making the Lord's-day a season of what is popularly called recreation, unnecessary travelling, personal convenience, or profit in temporal things, is, to us, perfectly shocking. We are of opinion that such acting could not be too severely censured. We can safely assert that we never yet came in contact with a godly, intelligent, right-minded Christian person who did not love and reverence the Lord's-day; nor could we have any sympathy with one who could deliberately desecrate that holy and happy day.

We are aware, alas! that some persons have, through ignorance or misguided feelings, said things in reference to the Lord's-day which we utterly repudiate, and that they have done things on the Lord's-day of which we wholly disapprove. We believe that there is a body of New Testament teaching on the important subject of the Lord's-day, quite sufficient to give that day its proper place in every well-regulated mind. The Lord Jesus rose from the dead on that day. (Matt. xxviii. 1—6; Mark xvi. 1, 2; Luke xxiv. 1; John xx. 1). He met His disciples, once and again, on that day. (John xx. 19, 26). The early disciples met to break bread on that day (Acts xx. 7). The apostle, by the Holy Ghost, directs the Corinthians to lay by their contributions for the poor on that day. (1 Cor. xvi. 2). And, finally, the exiled apostle was in the Spirit and received visions of the future on that day (Rev. i. 10). The above Scriptures are conclusive. They prove that the Lord's-day occupies a place quite unique, quite heavenly, quite divine. But they as fully prove the entire distinctness of the Jewish Sabbath and the Lord's-day. The two days are spoken of throughout the New Testament with fully as much distinctness as we speak of Saturday and Sunday. The only difference is, that the latter are heathen titles, and the former divine. (Comp. Matt. xxviii. 1; Acts xiii. 14, xvii. 2, xx. 7; Col. ii. 16.)

Having said thus much as to the question of the Jewish Sabbath and the Lord's-day, we shall suggest the following questions to the reader—namely, Where in the word of God is the sabbath said to be changed to the first day of the week? Where is there any repeal of the law as to the Sabbath? Where is the authority for altering the day or the mode of observing it? Where, in Scripture, have we such an expression as "the Christian Sabbath?" Where is the Lord's-day ever called the Sabbath? *

* For a fuller exposition of the doctrine of the Sabbath, see "Notes on Genesis" (chapter ii.). Also "Notes on Exodus" (chaps. xvi. & xxi.). London: George Morrish, 24, Warwick Lane, Paternoster Row.

We would not yield to any of our dear brethren in the various denominations around us, in the pious observance of the Lord's-day. We love and honour it with all our hearts ; and were it not that the gracious providence of God has so ordered it in these realms, that we can enjoy the rest and retirement of the Lord's-day without pecuniary loss, we should feel called upon to abstain from business, and give ourselves wholly up to the worship and service of God on that day, not as a matter of cold legality, but as a holy and happy privilege.

It would be the deepest sorrow to our hearts to think that a true Christian should be found taking common ground with the ungodly, the profane, the thoughtless, and the pleasure-hunting multitude, in desecrating the Lord's-day. It would be sad, indeed, if the children of the kingdom and the children of this world were to meet in an excursion train on the Lord's-day. We feel persuaded that any who, in any wise, profane or treat with lightness the Lord's-day, act in direct opposition to the word and Spirit of God.

The above are our thoughts in reference to the Lord's-day, and we therefore consider ourselves unfairly dealt with when we are represented as having any sympathy with the wickedness and infidelity that would propose measures for the open and deliberate profanation of the Lord's-day. We utterly abhor such measures and the spirit from which they emanate.

We shall now proceed to the consideration of the other points.

As regards the LAW, it is looked at in two ways: first, as the ground of justification; and secondly, as a rule of life. A passage or two of Scripture will suffice to settle both the one and the other. "Therefore by the deeds of the law there shall no flesh be justified in His sight: for by the law is the knowledge of sin" (Rom. iii. 20). "Therefore we conclude that a man is justified by faith without the deeds of the law" (ver. 28). Again, "Knowing that a man is not justified by the works of the law, but by the faith of Jesus Christ, even we have believed in Jesus Christ, that we might be justified by the faith of Christ, and not by the works of the law: for by the works of the law shall no flesh be justified" (Gal. ii. 16).

Then, as to its being a rule of life, we read, "Wherefore, my brethren, ye also are become dead to the law, by the body of Christ; that ye should be married to another, even to Him that is raised from the dead, that we should bring forth fruit unto God" (Rom. vii. 4). "But now are we delivered from the law, being dead to that [see margin] wherein we were held: that we should serve in newness of spirit, and not in the oldness of the letter" (ver. 6). Observe in this last-quoted passage, two things: 1st, "we are delivered from the law;" 2nd, not that we may do nature's pleasure, but "that we should *serve* in newness of spirit." Though delivered from bondage, it is our privilege to "serve" in liberty. Again, we read farther on in the chapter, "And the commandment which was ordained to life, I found to be *unto death*" (ver. 10). It evidently did not prove a rule of *life* to him. "I was *alive without the law* once: but *when the commandment came*, sin revived, and *I died*" (ver. 9). Whoever "I" represents in this chapter, was alive until the law came, and then he died. Hence, therefore, the law could not have been a rule of life to him; yea, it was the very opposite, even a rule of death.

In a word, then, it is evident that a sinner cannot be justified by the works of the law, and it is equally evident that the law is not the rule of the believer's life. "For as many as are of the works of the law are under the curse" (Gal. iii. 10). The law knows no such thing as a distinction between a regenerated and an unregenerated man; it curses all who attempt to stand before it. It rules and curses a man so long as he lives; nor is there any one who will so fully acknowledge that he cannot keep it as the true believer, and hence no one would be more thoroughly under the curse.

What, therefore, is the ground of our justification? and what is our rule of life? The word of God answers, "We are justified by the faith of Christ," and Christ is our rule of life. He bore all our sins in His own body on the tree; He was made a curse for us; He drained on our behalf the cup of God's righteous wrath; He deprived death of its sting, and the grave of its victory; He gave up His life for us: He went down into death, where we lay, in order that He might bring us up in eternal association with Himself in life, righteousness, favour, and glory, before our God and His God, our Father and His Father. (See carefully the following Scriptures: John xx. 17; Rom. iv. 25; v. 1–10; vi. 1–11; vii. *passim*, viii. 1–4; 1 Cor. i. 30, 31; vi. 11; xv. 55–57; 2 Cor. v. 17–21; Gal. iii. 13, 25–29; iv. 31; Eph. i. 19–23; ii. 1–6; Col. ii. 10–15; Heb. ii. 14, 15; 1 Pet. i. 23.) If the reader will prayerfully ponder all these passages of Scripture he will see clearly that we are not justified by the works of the law; and not only so, but he will see how we are justified. He will see the deep and solid foundations of the Christian's life, righteousness, and peace, planned in God's eternal counsels, laid in the finished atonement of Christ, developed by God the Holy Ghost in the word, and made good in the happy experience of all true believers.

Then, as to the believer's rule of life, the apostle does not say, To me to live is the law, but "To me to live is Christ" (Phil. i. 21). Christ is our rule, our model, our touchstone, our all. The continual inquiry of the Christian should be, not, Is this or that according to law? but, Is it like Christ? The law could never teach me to love, bless, and pray for my enemies; but this is exactly what the gospel teaches me to do, and what the divine nature leads me to do. "Love is the fulfilling of the law," and yet were I to seek justification by the law, I should be lost; and were I to make the law my standard of action, I should fall far short of my proper mark. We are predestinated to be conformed, not to the law, but to the image of God's Son. We are to be like Him. (See Matt. v. 21–48; Rom. viii. 29; 1 Cor. xiii. 4–8; Rom. xiii. 8–10; Gal: v. 14–26; Eph. i. 3–5; Phil. iii. 20, 21, ii. 5, iv. 8; Col. iii. 1–17.)

It may seem a paradox to some to be told that "the righteousness of the law is fulfilled in us" (Rom. viii. 4), and yet that we cannot be justified by the law, nor make the law our rule of life. Nevertheless, thus it is if we are to form our convictions by the word of God. Nor is there any difficulty to the renewed mind in understanding this blessed doctrine. We are, by nature, "dead in trespasses and sins," and what can a dead man do? How can a man get life by keeping that which requires life to keep it—a life which he has not? And how do we get life? Christ is our life. We live in Him who died for us; we are blessed in Him who became a curse for us by hanging on a tree; we are righteous in Him who was made sin for us; we are brought nigh to Him who was cast out for us (Rom. v. 6–15; Eph. ii. 4–6; Gal. iii. 13). Having thus life and righteousness in Christ, we are called to walk as He walked, and not merely to walk as a Jew. We are called to purify ourselves even as He is pure, to walk in His footsteps, to show forth His virtues, to manifest His spirit (John xiii. 14, 15; xvii. 14–19; 1 Pet. ii. 21; 1 John ii. 6, 29, iii. 3).

We shall close our remarks on this head by suggesting two questions to the reader, namely—Would the Ten Commandments without the New Testament be a sufficient rule of life for the believer? Would the New Testament be a sufficient rule without the Ten Commandments? Surely that which is insufficient cannot be our rule of life.

We receive the Ten Commandments as part of the canon of inspiration; and, moreover, we believe that the law remains in full force to rule and curse a man as long as he liveth. Let a sinner only try to get life by it, and see where it will put him; and let a believer only shape his way according to it, and see what it will make of him. We are fully convinced that if a man is walking according to the spirit of the gospel, he will not commit murder nor steal; but we are also convinced, that a man, confining himself to the standard of the law of Moses, would fall very far short of the spirit of the gospel.

The subject of "the law" would demand much more elaborate exposition, but the limits of this paper will not admit of it, and we therefore entreat of the reader to look out for the various passages of Scripture referred to and ponder them carefully. In this way we feel assured he will arrive at a sound conclusion, and be independent of all human teaching and influence. He will see how that a man is justified freely by the grace of God, through faith in a crucified and risen Christ; that he is made a partaker of divine life, and introduced into a condition of divine and everlasting righteousness, and consequent exemption from all condemnation; that in this holy and elevated position, Christ is his object, his theme, his model, his rule, his hope, his joy, his strength, his all; that the hope which is set before him is to be with Jesus where He is, and to be like Him for ever. And he will also see that if, as a lost sinner, he has found pardon and peace at the foot of the Cross, he is not, as an accepted and adopted son, sent back to the foot of mount Sinai, there to be terrified and repulsed by the terrible anathemas of a broken law. The Father could not think of ruling with an iron law the prodigal whom He had received to His bosom in purest, deepest, richest grace. Oh! no; "being justified by faith we have peace with God, through our Lord Jesus Christ; by whom also we have access by faith into this GRACE wherein we stand, and rejoice in hope of the glory of God" (Rom. v. 1, 2). The believer is justified not by works, but by *faith;* he stands not in law, but in *grace;* and he waits not for judgment, but for *glory.*

We now come, in the third place, to treat of the subject of the CHRISTIAN MINISTRY, in reference to which we have only to say, that we hold it to be a Divine institution—its source, its power, its characteristics are all divine and heavenly. We believe that the great Head of the Church received, in resurrection, gifts for His body. He, and not the Church, or any section of the Church, is the reservoir of the gifts. They are vested in Him, and not in the Church. He imparts them as and to whom He will. No man nor body of men can impart gifts. This is Christ's prerogative, and His alone; and we believe that when He imparts a gift, the man who receives that gift is responsible to exercise the same, whether as an evangelist, a pastor, or a teacher, quite independently of all human authority.

We do not by any means believe that all are endowed with the above gifts, though all have some ministry to fulfil. All are not evangelists, pastors, and teachers. Such precious gifts are only administered according to the sovereign will of the divine Head of the Church. Man has no right to interfere with them. Wherever they really exist, it is the place of the assembly to recognise them with devout thankfulness. Christians are exhorted to remember them that are over them in the Lord, to know them that guide them, and those who addict themselves to the ministry of the saints, and those who have spoken to them the word of life. Were they to refuse to do so, they would only be forsaking and rejecting their own mercies, for all things are theirs. (See Rom. xii. 3—8; 1 Cor. iii. 21—23; xii., xiv., xvi. 15; Gal. i. 11—17; Eph. iv. 7—16; 1 Thess. v. 12, 13; Heb. xiii. 7, 17; 1 Pet. iv. 10, 11.)

All this is simple enough. We can easily see where a man is divinely qualified for any department of ministry. It is not if a man *say* he has a gift, but if he in reality has it. A man may say he has a gift on the same principle as he may say he has faith (Jas. ii. 14), and it may only be, after all, an empty conceit of his own ill-adjusted mind, which a spiritual assembly could not recognise for a moment. God deals in realities. A divinely gifted evangelist is a reality; a teacher is a reality; a pastor is a reality; and such will be duly recognised, thankfully received, and counted worthy of all esteem and honour for their work's sake.

Now, we hold that, unless a man has a *bonâ fide* gift imparted to him by the Head of the Church, all the instruction, all the education, and all the training that men could impart to him would not constitute him a Christian minister. If a man has a gift, he is responsible to exercise, to cultivate, and to wait upon his gift. Such an one may or may not be extensively read in human literature; he may or he may not be able to enlist his extensive reading in the Master's service. But, clearly, if a man has *only* the qualifications which human literature, human science, and human culture can impart, he is no more competent to be a Christian minister than a self-constituted quack is entitled to be regarded by the faculty of medicine as a duly-recognised practitioner.

Let us not be misunderstood. We hold that unless a man has a direct gift from Christ, though he had all the learning of a Newton, all the philosophy of a Bacon, all the eloquence of a Demosthenes, he is not a Christian minister. He may be a very gifted and efficient minister of religion, so-called; but a minister of religion and a minister of Christ are two different things. And, further, we believe that where the Lord Christ has bestowed a gift, that gift makes the possessor thereof a Christian minister, whom all true Christians are bound to own and receive, quite apart from all human appointment. Whereas, though a man had all the human qualifications, human titles, and human authority which it is possible to possess, and yet lacked that one grand reality, namely, Christ's gift, he is not a minister of Christ.

Such is our judgment in reference to the divine institution of the ministry; and hence, it is not fair or candid to accuse us of throwing that institution overboard. God forbid! We bless His name for Christian ministry; and we feel assured that there are many truly gifted servants of Christ in the various denominations around us; but they are ministers of Christ, on the ground of possessing His gift, and not, by any means, on the ground of man's ordination. Man cannot add aught to a heaven-bestowed gift. As well might he attempt to add a shade to the rainbow, a tint to the violet, motion to the waves, height to the snow-capped mountains, or daub with a painter's brush the peacock's plumage, as attempt to render more efficient, by his puny authority, the gift which has come down from the risen and glorified Head of the Church. Ah, no! the vine, the olive, and the fig-tree, in Jotham's parable (Jud. ix.), needed not the appointment of the other trees. God had implanted in each its specific virtue. It was only the worthless bramble which hailed with delight an appointment that raised it from the position of *a real nothing* to be *an official something*. Thus it is with a divinely gifted man. He has what God has given him; he wants, he asks no more. He rises above the narrow enclosures which man's authority would erect around him, and plants his foot upon that elevated ground where prophets and apostles have stood. He feels that it lies not within the range of the schools and colleges of this world, to open to him his proper sphere of action. It appertains not to them to provide a setting for the precious gem which sovereign grace has imparted. The Hand which has bestowed the gem can alone provide the proper setting. The grace which has implanted the gift can alone throw open a proper sphere for its exercise. What! can it be possible that those gifts that emanate from the Church's triumphant and glorious Lord are not available for her edification, until they are dragged through the mire of a heathen mythology? Alas! for the heart that can think so. As well might we say that the fatness of the olive and the pure blood of the grape must be mingled with the contents of a quagmire, to render them available for human use.

But, it will be asked, "Were there not elders

and deacons in the early Church, and ought we not to have such likewise?" Unquestionably, there were elders and deacons in the early Church. They were appointed by the apostles, or those whom the apostles deputed. That is to say, they were appointed by the Holy Ghost, the only One who could then or can now appoint them. We believe that none but God can make or appoint an elder; and, therefore, for man to set about such work is but a powerless form, an empty name. Men may and do point us to the shadows of their own creation, and call upon us to recognise in those shadows divine realities; but, alas! when we examine them in the light of Holy Scripture, we cannot even trace the outline, to say nothing of the living, speaking, features of the divine original. We see divinely appointed elders in the New Testament, and we see humanly appointed elders in the professing church; but we can by no means accept the latter as a substitute for the former. We cannot accept a mere shadow in lieu of the substance. Neither do we believe that men have any Divine authority for their act when they set about making and appointing elders. We believe that when Paul or Timothy or Titus ordained elders, they did so as acting by the power and under the direct authority of the Holy Ghost; but we deny that any man, or body of men, can so act now. We believe it was the Holy Ghost then, and it must be the Holy Ghost now. Human assumption is perfectly contemptible. If God raises up an elder or a pastor we thankfully own him. He both can and does raise up such. He does raise up men fitted, by His Spirit, to take the oversight of His flock, and to feed His lambs and sheep. His hand is not shortened that He cannot provide those blessings for His Church, even amid its humiliating ruins. The reservoir of spiritual gift in Christ, the Head, is not so exhausted that He cannot shed forth upon His body all that is needed for the edification thereof. We are of opinion that, were it not for our impatient attempts to provide for ourselves, by making pastors and elders of our own, we should be far more richly endowed with pastors and teachers after God's own heart. We need not marvel that He leaves us to our own resources when, by our unbelief, we limit Him in His. Instead of "proving" Him we "limit" Him; and, therefore, we are shorn of our strength, and left in barrenness and desolation; or, what is worse, we betake ourselves to the miserable provisions of human expediency. However, we believe it is far better, if we have not God's reality, to remain in the position of real, felt, confessed weakness, than to put forth the hollow assumption of strength; we believe it is better to be real in our poverty than to put on the appearance of wealth. It is infinitely better to wait on God for whatever He may be pleased to bestow, than to limit His grace by our unbelief, or hinder His provision for us by making provision for ourselves.

We ask, where is the Church's warrant for

calling, making, or appointing pastors? Where have we an instance in the New Testament of a Church electing its own pastor? Acts i. 23—26 has been adduced in proof. But the very wording of the passage is sufficient to prove that it furnishes no warrant whatsoever. Even the eleven apostles could not elect a brother apostle, but had to commit it to higher authority. Their words are—"THOU, LORD, *which knowest the hearts of all*, show whether of these two *Thou hast chosen*." This is very plain. They did not attempt to choose. God knew the heart. He had formed the vessel. He had put the treasure therein, and He alone could appoint it to its proper place.

It is very evident, therefore, that the case of the eleven apostles calling upon the Lord to choose a man to fill up their number, affords no precedent whatever for a congregation electing a pastor; it is entirely against any such practice. God alone can make or appoint an apostle or an elder, an evangelist or a pastor. This is our firm belief, and we ask for a Scripture proof of its unsoundness. Human opinion will not avail; tradition will not avail; expediency will not avail. Let us be taught from the word of God, that the early Church ever elected its own pastors or teachers. We positively affirm that there is not so much as a single line of Scripture in proof of any such custom. If we could only find direction in the word of God to make and appoint pastors, we should at once seek to carry such direction into effect; but, in the absence of any Divine warrant, we could only regard it as a mimicry, on our part, to attempt such a thing. Why was not the Church at Ephesus, or why were not the Churches at Crete directed to elect or appoint elders? Why was the direction given to Timothy and Titus, without the slightest reference to the Church or to any part of the Church? Because, as we believe, Timothy and Titus acted by the direct power and under the direct authority of God the Holy Ghost, and hence their appointment was to be regarded by the Church as Divine.*

* We would here offer a remark in reference to the appointment of deacons in Acts vi. This case has been adduced in proof of the rightness of a congregation electing its own pastor; but the proof fails in every particular. In the first place, the business of those deacons was "to serve tables." Their functions as deacons were temporal, not spiritual. They might possess spiritual gift, independently altogether of their deaconship. Stephen did possess such.

But more than this. Although the disciples were called upon to look out for men competent to take charge of their temporal affairs, yet the apostles alone could appoint them. Their words are, "Whom *we* may appoint over this business." In other words, although there is a vast difference between a deacon and a pastor, between taking charge of money and taking the oversight of souls, yet even in the matter of a deacon, the appointment in Acts vi. was entirely Divine; and hence it affords no warrant for a Church electing its own pastor.

We might further add, that *office* and *gift* are clearly distinguished in the word of God. There might be, and were, many elders and deacons in any given Church, and yet the fullest and freest exercise of gift when the whole Church came

But where have we anything like this now? Where is the Timothy or the Titus now? Where is there the least intimation in the New Testament that there should be a succession of men invested with the power to ordain elders or pastors? True, the Apostle Paul, in his Second Epistle to Timothy, says, "The things which thou hast heard of me among many witnesses, the same commit thou to faithful men, who shall be able to teach others also" (2 Tim. ii. 2). But there is not a word here about a succession of men having power to ordain elders and pastors. Assuredly teaching is not ordination, still less is it imparting the power to ordain. If the inspired apostle had meant to convey to the mind of Timothy that he was to commit to others authority to ordain, and that such authority was to descend by a regular chain of succession, he could and would have done so, and in that case, the passage would have run thus: "The power which has been vested in you, the same do thou vest in faithful men, that they may be able also to ordain others." Such, however, is not the case; and we deny that there is any man, or body of men, now upon earth, possessing power to ordain elders, nor was that power or authority

together into one place. Elders and deacons might or might not have the gift of teaching or exhortation. Such gift was quite independent of their special office. In 1 Corinthians xiv., where it is said, "Ye may all prophesy one by one," and where we have a full view of the public assembly, there is not a word about an elder or a president of any kind whatever.

ever committed to the Church. We hold it to be absolutely Divine, and therefore, when God sends an elder or a pastor, an evangelist or a teacher, we thankfully hail the heaven-bestowed gift; but we desire to be delivered from all empty pretension. We will have God's reality or nothing. We will have heaven's genuine coin, not earth's counterfeit. Like the Tirshatha of old who said "that they should not eat of the most holy things till there stood up a priest with Urim and Thummim" (Ez. ii. 63), so would we say, let us rather, if it must be so, remain without office-bearers than substitute for God's realities the shadows of our own creation. Ezra could not accept the pretensions of men. Men might *say* they were priests, but if they could not produce the Divine warrant and the Divine qualifications, they were utterly rejected. In order for a man to be entitled to approach the altar of the God of Israel, he should not only be descended from Aaron, but also be free from every bodily blemish. (See Lev. xxi. 16–23.) So now, in order for any man to minister in the Church of God, he must be a regenerated man, and he must have the necessary spiritual qualifications. Even St. Paul in his powerful appeal to the conscience and judgment of the Church at Corinth, refers to his spiritual gifts and the fruits of his labour, as the indisputable evidences of his apostleship. (See 2 Cor. x., xii.)

Before dismissing the subject of the Christian

ministry, we would offer a remark upon the practice of laying on of hands, which is presented in the New Testament in two ways.

First, we find it connected with the communication of a positive gift. "Neglect not the gift that is in thee, which was given thee by prophecy, with the laying on of the hands of the presbytery" (1 Tim. iv. 14). This is again referred to in the second epistle: "Wherefore I put thee in remembrance that thou stir up the gift of God, which is in thee by the putting on of my hands" (2 Tim. i. 6). This latter passage fixes the import of the expression "presbytery," as used in the first epistle. Both passages prove that the act of laying on of hands, in Timothy's case, was connected with the imparting of a gift.

But, secondly, we find the laying on of hands adopted simply for the purpose of expressing full fellowship and identification, as in Acts xiii. 3. It could not possibly mean ordination in this passage, inasmuch as Paul and Barnabas had been in the ministry long before. It simply gave beautiful expression to the full identification of their brethren in that work unto which the Holy Ghost had called them, and to which He alone could send them forth.

Now, we believe that the laying on of hands, as expressing ordination, if there be not the power to impart a gift, is worth nothing, if indeed it be not mere assumption; but if it be merely adopted as the expression of full fellowship in any special work or mission, we should quite rejoice in it. For example, if two or three brethren felt themselves called of God to go on an evangelistic mission to the United States of America, and those with whom they were in communion perceived in them the needed gift and grace for such a work, we should deem it exceedingly happy were they to set forth their unqualified approval and their brotherly fellowship by the act of laying on of hands. Beyond this we can see no value whatever in that act.

Having thus, so far as our limits would permit, treated of the questions of the Sabbath, the Law, and the Christian Ministry—having shown that we honour and observe the Lord's-day, that we give the Law its Divinely appointed place, and, finally, that we hold the sacred and precious institution of the Christian Ministry, we might close this paper, did we not feel called upon to meet another charge which is frequently preferred against us—viz., the maintenance of a Jesuitical reserve in reference to our peculiar opinions until such time as we have persons under our influence. This charge is totally unfounded.

In our general teaching and preaching, we seek to set forth the fundamental truths of the gospel, such as the doctrine of the Trinity, the eternal Sonship, the personality of the Holy Ghost, the plenary inspiration of Holy Scripture, the eternal counsels of God in reference to His elect, and yet the fullest and freest presentation of His love to a ost world; the solemn responsibility of every one who hears the glad tidings of salvation to accept the same; man's total ruin by nature and by practice; his inability to help himself in thought, word, or deed; the utter corruption of his will; Christ's incarnation, death, and resurrection; His absolute deity and perfect humanity in one person; the perfect efficacy of His blood to cleanse from all sin; perfect justification and sanctification by faith in Christ, through the operation of God the Holy Ghost; the eternal security of all true believers; the entire separation of the Church in calling, standing, and hope, from this present world.

Then, again, we hold, in common with many of our brethren in the Church of England and in the Free Church of Scotland, that the hope of the believer is set forth in these words of Christ: "I will come again and receive you unto myself; that where I am there ye may be also" (John xiv. 3). We believe that the early Christians were converted to "that blessed hope;" that it was the common hope of Christians in apostolic times. To adduce proofs would swell this paper into a volume.

Furthermore, we believe that all the disciples should meet on the first day of the week to break bread (Acts xx. 7), and when so met, they should look to the Head of the Church to furnish the needed gifts, and to the Holy Ghost to guide in the due administration of these gifts.

As to the scriptural ordinance of baptism, we look upon it as a beautiful exhibition of the truth that the believer is associated with Christ in death and resurrection. (See Matt. xxviii. 19; Mark xvi. 16; Acts ii. 38, 41; viii. 38; x. 47, 48; xvi. 33; Rom. vi. 3, 4.)

As regards the precious institution of the Lord's Supper, we believe that Christians should celebrate it on every Lord's-day, and that, in so doing, they commemorate the Lord's death until He come. We believe that as baptism sets forth our death with Christ, so the Lord's Supper sets forth Christ's death for us. We do not see any authority in the word of God for regarding the Lord's Supper as "a sacrifice," "a sacrament," or "a covenant." The word is, "This do in remembrance of me." (See Matt. xxvi. 26, 28; Mark xiv. 22–24; Luke xxii. 19, 20; 1 Cor. xi. 23–26.)

The above is a very brief but explicit statement of our opinions and our practice; and we affectionately ask the candid and judicious reader where is there aught of the Jesuit therein? We meet in public, our worship meetings, our prayer meetings, our reading meetings, our lectures, our gospel preachings, are all open to the public.

No intelligent person could suppose that we ought, in preaching the gospel to the unconverted, to introduce the deeper mysteries of the kingdom of heaven, or the Church of God. The Lord Jesus spake the word to the people "as they were able to hear it" (Mark iv. 33). The Holy Ghost, by the apostle, did the same (1 Cor. iii. 1, 2; Heb. v. 11–14). Should not every judicious teacher adapt his instructions to the condition of the taught? Who would teach conic sections or Euclid's elements to a child who had only learnt his alphabet? It must at all times be a question of spiritual wisdom as to what character of truth one ought to bring before those with whom he comes in contact; and it may sometimes be a question of grace to withhold a topic which would only produce controversy and hinder Christian fellowship; but surely wisdom and grace ought not to be dubbed with the opprobrious epithet of Jesuitical reserve.

But we have done. We would, in this closing line, entreat the reader to "search the Scriptures." Let him try everything by that standard. Let him see to it that he has plain Scripture for everything with which he stands connected. "To the law and to the testimony: if they speak not according to this word, it is because there is no light in them" (Isa. viii. 20).

We now commend the reader to the blessing of the Father and of the Son and of the Holy Ghost. If he be a true believer, we pray that, in his course down here, he may be a bright and faithful witness for his absent Lord. But if he be one who has not yet found peace in Jesus, we would say to him, with solemn emphasis and earnest affection, "BEHOLD THE LAMB OF GOD, WHICH TAKETH AWAY THE SIN OF THE WORLD" (John i. 29).

4, CHURCH STREET, COLERAINE,
October, 1857.

Butler & Tanner, The Selwood Printing Works, Frome, and London.

LaVergne, TN USA
03 May 2010
181282LV00003B/119/P

9 781141 497904